MENTAL EXERCISES FOR DOGS

The Most Comprehensive Guide to Stimulate Your Dog's Brain, Build a Stronger Bond, and Enhance Emotional Connection with the Best 101 Fun & Interactive Games

Ivana Dorothea

Table of Content

Introduction 5

Chapter 1
Mutual Learning 7

Evolution of Canine Companionship 7
Dogs in Modern Urban Life 9

Chapter 1
How is your Dog? 15

Small and Medium-Sized Dogs for Urban Living 15
French Bulldog 15
Pug 16
Cavalier King Charles Spaniel 16
Boston Terrier 17
Miniature Schnauzer 17
Shetland Sheepdog (Sheltie) 18
Bichon Frise 19
Cocker Spaniel 19
Choosing the Right Breed for Your Urban Lifestyle 20
Understanding Canine Intelligence 22
Tailoring Exercises to Stimulate Specific Intelligence Areas .. 26

Chapter 2
How to Make your Dog Play 29

The Essential Guide to Carefree Playtime with Your Canine Companion ... 31
Food Games 32
Hunting Games 38
Scent Games 44
Agility And Balancing Games 50
Water Games 56
Focus Games 61
Impulse Control Games 66
Mental Health And Cognitive Games 71
Indoor And Outdoor Games 77
Teaching To Play With Kids 82
Measuring Progress and Adjusting Your Dog's Mental Stimulation Routine ... 88

BONUS
The best 5 recipes for the health of your dog friend 91

Chapter 3
Conclusion 93

Introduction

Welcome to the world of dog ownership, a journey filled with joy, companionship, and the boundless energy of our four-legged friends. As a dog owner myself, I've come to realize that having a furry companion isn't just about walks in the park or cuddles on the couch; it's about fostering a relationship built on trust, love, and mutual understanding.

The main objective of this book is simple yet crucial: to help you cultivate an active, healthy lifestyle for your dog—one that goes beyond mere physical activity to encompass mental engagement, socialization, and bonding with you, your family, and even other pets. Dogs, much like humans, thrive on mental stimulation and social interaction. They crave challenges, new experiences, and opportunities to learn and grow. By incorporating a variety of mental exercises into your dog's routine, you can provide them with the mental enrichment they need to lead fulfilling lives.

Throughout these pages, you'll discover a plethora of activities designed to engage your dog's mind and keep them entertained for hours on end. From interactive games and puzzle toys to obedience training and sensory enrichment exercises, each activity is crafted with your dog's well-being and happiness in mind. Whether you have a curious pup eager to explore the world or a senior dog looking to keep their mind sharp, there's something here for every canine companion.

But this book isn't just about keeping your dog entertained—it's also about fostering meaningful connections between you and your furry friend. Dogs are incredibly social creatures, and they thrive on the companionship and love of their human families. By engaging in activities together, whether it's a game of hide-and-seek or a training session at the park, you'll strengthen your bond with your dog and create memories that will last a lifetime.

One aspect I particularly want to emphasize is the role that children can play in caring for and interacting with dogs. Growing up with a dog can be a transformative experience for children, teaching them valuable lessons in responsibility, empathy, and compassion. By involving children in the care and training of the family dog, we not only instill in them a sense of responsibility but also nurture a lifelong love and respect for animals.

In the following chapters, we'll explore a wide range of mental exercises and activities tailored to suit dogs of all ages, breeds, and temperaments. Whether you're looking to challenge your dog's problem-solving skills, boost their confidence, or simply provide them with some mental stimulation on a rainy day, you'll find plenty of inspiration and guidance here.

Remember that the key to a happy, healthy dog lies not just in meeting their physical needs but also in nourishing their minds and souls. So grab a treat, gather your pup, and let's dive into the wonderful world of mental exercises for dogs. Together, we'll unlock the full potential of our canine companions and create a lifetime of cherished memories along the way.

Chapter 1
Mutual Learning

The story of human-dog companionship is a tale as old as time, a narrative written across centuries in the shared history of two species bound by an unspoken connection. From the dusty trails of ancient civilizations to the bustling streets of modern urban life, the evolution of this partnership is a fascinating journey that has shaped both humans and dogs. In this chapter, we embark on a journey through time, tracing the footsteps of our canine companions from their wild origins to the cherished members of our families today.

Evolution of Canine Companionship

The bond between humans and dogs is one of the oldest and most enduring relationships in history. Tracing back to ancient civilizations, this companionship has evolved from a utilitarian relationship based on hunting and protection to a deep emotional connection that enriches the lives of both species. Dogs, once wild animals, have been transformed into beloved companions, serving diverse roles in human society and becoming an integral part of our lives.

Ancient Beginnings

The history of dogs as companions to humans can be traced back thousands of years. One of the earliest known records of this bond comes from ancient Egypt, where dogs were revered for their loyalty and hunting prowess. They were depicted in tombs and on artifacts, often accompanying their human counterparts in the afterlife. In ancient Mesopotamia, dogs were valued for their ability to protect livestock and homes from predators, with mentions of them as guardians in ancient texts.

Moving further back, to the Paleolithic era, the relationship between humans and dogs likely began as a mutually beneficial partnership. As nomadic hunter-gatherer societies emerged, dogs proved invaluable as hunting aids. Their keen senses and agility made them indispensable for tracking and capturing prey, significantly increasing the success of early human hunters. Archaeological evidence suggests that this partnership dates back at least 20,000 years, with early humans domesticating wolves to create the first proto-dogs.

Evolution from Wild to Domesticated

The transition from wild wolves to domesticated dogs marked a significant turning point in the history of this relationship. Over generations of selective breeding, humans shaped the physical and behavioral traits of dogs to better suit various roles. Initially, these roles were primarily utilitarian, focusing on hunting, herding, and guarding.

In ancient China, for example, dogs were selectively bred for specific tasks. The Chow Chow, with its distinctive blue-black tongue, was used for hunting and guarding, while the Pekingese was a cherished companion of the imperial court. Meanwhile, in the Roman Empire, large Mastiffs were used as war dogs, feared for their strength and ferocity in battle.

Dogs in Historical Moments

Throughout history, dogs have played pivotal roles in shaping the course of human events. In medieval Europe, for instance, they were indispensable for hunting, a popular pastime among nobility. Breeds like the Scottish Deerhound were prized for their ability to track and bring down game, while smaller breeds such as the Cocker Spaniel were adept at flushing out birds.

One of the most famous dogs in history is undoubtedly "Balto," a Siberian Husky who was in charge of the last leg of the serum run that took place in 1925 to Nome, Alaska. When an outbreak of diphtheria threatened the remote town, a relay of dog sled teams, led by Balto and his musher Gunnar Kaasen, braved blizzard conditions to deliver life-saving medicine. Balto's heroism captured the world's attention, immortalizing him as a symbol of courage and loyalty.

During wartime, dogs have served as loyal companions and invaluable assets on the battlefield. In World War I, "war dogs" were used for a variety of tasks, from carrying messages to detecting mines. The most famous war dog of this era was "Sgt. Stubby," a mixed-breed terrier who served with the American Expeditionary Forces. Stubby's keen sense of smell and hearing helped save countless lives by warning of impending gas attacks and locating wounded soldiers on the battlefield.

Modern Roles and Companionship

In contemporary society, dogs have transcended their traditional roles to become cherished family members and emotional support companions. The concept of "man's best friend" has taken on new meaning as dogs provide unconditional love, companionship, and emotional support to their human counterparts.

Therapy dogs, for example, play a vital role in improving the well-being of individuals in hospitals, nursing homes, and schools. Their calming presence and innate ability to connect with people provide comfort during times of stress and uncertainty. Furthermore, service dogs are taught to aid people who have impairments. They are able to do a variety of jobs, such as guiding people who have difficulty seeing and warning people who have medical issues of imminent health crises.

The advent of dog sports and competitions further demonstrates the versatility and intelligence of these remarkable animals. From agility trials to obedience competitions, dogs showcase their athleticism, discipline, and willingness to work alongside their human handlers. Breeds like the Border Collie excel in herding trials, demonstrating their innate herding instincts and intelligence.

The evolution of canine companionship is a testament to the enduring bond between humans and dogs. From ancient civilizations where they served as hunting partners and guardians to modern times where they provide emotional support and assistance, dogs have played diverse and vital roles in our lives. Their loyalty, intelligence, and unwavering devotion continue to enrich the human experience, reminding us of the profound connection between our species. As we look back on the historical journey of this remarkable relationship, one thing remains clear: dogs truly are "man's best friend."

Dogs in Modern Urban Life

As humanity has transitioned from agrarian societies to bustling urban landscapes, so too has the role of dogs evolved. Once indispensable for hunting, herding, and guarding, dogs now find themselves as integral members of households amidst skyscrapers and concrete sidewalks.

Shifting Objectives of Dog Ownership

The relationship between humans and dogs has undergone a remarkable transformation over the centuries, evolving from practical and utilitarian purposes to deeply emotional and companionship-driven bonds. In the context of modern urban life, this shift is particularly evident, as dogs are increasingly valued for their roles as companions, emotional support providers, and even family members.

Companionship and Emotional Support

Perhaps the most profound change in the objectives of dog ownership in urban settings is the emphasis on companionship and emotional support. In a world where individuals can feel isolated despite being surrounded by millions, dogs offer a unique kind of solace. They are unwaveringly present, providing a sense of comfort and companionship that transcends words.

In urban apartments or bustling city streets, where the pace of life can be relentless, dogs offer a calming influence. Their mere presence can reduce stress levels, lower blood pressure, and elevate mood. Research has shown that petting a dog releases oxytocin, the "love hormone," promoting feelings of happiness and well-being. This emotional bond between humans and dogs is not merely a luxury but has become a necessity for many urban dwellers seeking solace in the chaos of city life.

Social Connectors and Community Builders

In the sprawling metropolises where anonymity can be the norm, dogs serve as powerful social connectors. Urban dog parks have become modern-day gathering spots, where neighbors meet, friendships form, and community bonds strengthen. The shared experience of caring for these furry companions creates a sense of camaraderie, breaking down the barriers that often exist between strangers.

Walking a dog down city streets is not just a routine exercise; it's an opportunity for connection. Conversations spark easily between dog owners, exchanging tips on training techniques, sharing stories of antics, or simply commiserating over the challenges of urban pet ownership. Through these interactions, neighborhoods become more than just a collection of buildings; they become vibrant communities united by a love for their four-legged residents.

Playmates and Exercise Partners

Urban life can often be sedentary, with long hours spent indoors or in office buildings. Dogs provide a powerful incentive to step outside, breathe fresh air, and engage in physical activity. Whether it's a brisk walk around the block, a jog through a nearby park, or a game of fetch in designated dog areas, these activities benefit both dog and owner alike. The need for regular exercise is met with enthusiasm by dogs, who are always eager for adventure and exploration. For urbanites, this means a healthier lifestyle, improved fitness, and a natural antidote to the stresses of city living. Dogs not only encourage physical activity but also add an element of joy and spontaneity to daily routines, making each outing an adventure.

Protectors and Guardians

In cities where safety concerns can weigh heavily on residents, dogs offer a sense of security. Their keen senses and natural instincts make them excellent watchdogs, alerting owners to any unusual sounds or visitors. Even small breeds, known more for their cuddly demeanor than intimidating stature, offer a sense of safety when walking alone at night or residing in urban apartments.

Beyond their role as protectors of property, dogs also serve as guardians of their human companions' emotional well-being. Many urban residents report feeling safer and more secure knowing their faithful canine companions are by their side, ready to alert them to any potential threats or dangers.

In the dynamic and diverse landscape of urban environments, dogs seamlessly adapt to a myriad of roles, enriching the lives of their owners and the communities they inhabit. From providing therapeutic companionship to serving as service animals, environmental guardians, and even social media influencers, dogs play diverse and varied roles that reflect the complexities of modern urban life.

Multifaceted Roles of Dogs in Urban Settings

In the dynamic and diverse landscape of urban environments, dogs seamlessly adapt to a myriad of roles, enriching the lives of their owners and the communities they inhabit. From providing therapeutic companionship to serving as service animals, environmental guardians, and even social media influencers, dogs play diverse and varied roles that reflect the complexities of modern urban life.

Therapeutic Companions

One of the most notable roles dogs play in urban settings is that of therapeutic companions. In a world where stress and anxiety are pervasive, dogs offer a source of comfort and emotional support to their human counterparts. This is particularly evident in settings such as hospitals, nursing homes, and therapy centers, where trained therapy dogs provide comfort and companionship to patients facing illness or adversity. Studies have indicated that engagements with therapy dogs lead to decreased anxiety and depression, reduced blood pressure, and an overall enhancement in well-being. The non-judgmental companionship they provide establishes a secure environment for people to freely express themselves and form deeper connections with others. This becomes particularly significant in urban settings where mental health services might be scarce, as therapy dogs serve as a precious source of comfort and support for individuals seeking solace.

Service and Assistance Dogs

In urban settings, dogs play diverse roles beyond being companions, often serving as indispensable service animals for individuals with disabilities. Guide dogs, for instance, offer vital aid to the visually impaired, guiding them through bustling city streets and fostering a sense of independence and mobility. Meanwhile, hearing dogs play a crucial role by alerting their owners to significant sounds amidst the urban noise, such as approaching vehicles or emergency sirens, thereby enhancing safety and awareness.

Service dogs are extensively trained to support individuals with mobility impairments, offering assistance with tasks such as opening doors, retrieving items, and navigating obstacles. Particularly in urban environments where accessibility poses challenges, these expertly trained dogs provide invaluable aid, empowering their human partners to confidently navigate the complexities of city life with autonomy.

Environmental Guardians

Amidst concerns of pollution and environmental degradation in urban areas, dogs have emerged as guardians of green spaces, tasked with protecting the natural world from harm. K9 units employed by environmental agencies are trained to detect harmful substances, such as illegal drugs or pollutants, in parks and public areas. These dogs play a vital role in preserving the integrity of urban ecosystems, ensuring that public spaces remain safe and healthy for both humans and wildlife.

In addition to their roles in law enforcement, environmental dogs are also employed in conservation efforts, sniffing out endangered species, detecting invasive species, and tracking wildlife populations. Their remarkable sense of smell and boundless energy make them indispensable allies in the fight to protect and preserve urban biodiversity, ensuring that forthcoming generations can continue to enjoy the natural beauty of city parks and green spaces.

Celebrity Canines and Social Media Influencers

In the age of social media, certain dogs have risen to stardom, amassing millions of followers and becoming influencers in their own right. From Instagram-famous pooches to canine YouTubers, these dogs capture the hearts and imaginations of urban dwellers worldwide, offering entertainment, inspiration, and a daily dose of cuteness to their legions of fans.

These celebrity canines often serve as ambassadors for pet adoption, charitable causes, and environmental awareness, using their platforms to advocate for positive change in the world. Through partnerships with brands and organizations, they raise awareness and funds for important causes, leveraging their popularity for the greater good. In an era where social media can sometimes feel overwhelming, these furry influencers offer a welcome respite, spreading joy and positivity to millions of followers around the globe.

Challenges of Urban Dog Ownership

While the benefits of having a canine companion in urban settings are plentiful, there are also unique challenges that dog owners must navigate. From limited living space to finding suitable exercise areas and ensuring proper socialization, urban dog ownership requires careful consideration and planning. Let's delve into some of the key challenges faced by those who choose to share their city lives with furry friends.

Space Limitations

One of the most apparent challenges of urban dog ownership is the issue of space. Many city dwellers live in apartments or condominiums with limited square footage, leaving little room for pets to roam freely. This is especially true for larger dog breeds, whose size may exceed the allowable limits set by landlords or building management.

For owners of large breeds such as Great Danes or Saint Bernards, finding suitable housing can be a daunting task. Many rental properties have weight or size restrictions on pets, making it challenging to find a pet-friendly apartment that accommodates larger dogs. This often leads to a trade-off between the desire for a spacious living environment and the love for a particular breed.

Even for owners of smaller breeds, space constraints can be an issue. Dogs need room to move, play, and explore, and cramped living quarters can lead to boredom and behavioral issues. Without adequate space to stretch their legs and burn off energy, dogs may become restless, leading to excessive barking, chewing, or other destructive behaviors.

Exercise and Activity Needs

Urban environments can present challenges when it comes to meeting a dog's exercise and activity requirements. While cities offer access to parks and green spaces, these areas may be limited in size or overcrowded, especially during peak times. This can make it difficult for dogs to run and play freely, leading to a lack of adequate exercise.

Additionally, not all urban areas have designated dog parks or off-leash areas, forcing owners to seek out alternative options for exercise. This may involve driving to nearby parks or traveling to suburban areas, which can be time-consuming and inconvenient for busy city dwellers.

The need for regular exercise is crucial for a dog's physical health and mental well-being. Without proper outlets for physical activity, dogs may become lethargic, overweight, or develop behavioral problems. Owners must make a concerted effort to provide daily exercise routines, whether through walks, runs, or play sessions, to ensure their furry companions remain healthy and happy.

Socialization Opportunities

Proper socialization is essential for dogs to become well-adjusted members of society, but urban environments can present unique challenges in this regard. The constant stimuli of city life, including loud noises, crowded streets, and unfamiliar sights and smells, can be overwhelming for some dogs, especially puppies or those with timid personalities.

Limited access to other dogs for socialization can also be a challenge in urban settings. While dog parks and pet-friendly establishments offer opportunities for interaction, these spaces may not always be accessible or suitable for every dog. Some owners may find it challenging to coordinate playdates or meetups with other dog owners due to busy schedules or conflicting commitments.

A lack of proper socialization can lead to behavioral issues such as fearfulness, aggression, or excessive shyness in dogs. It is essential for owners to expose their pets to a variety of environments, people, and animals from an early age to build confidence and positive social skills.

Time Commitment

Owning a dog in an urban environment requires a significant time commitment from owners. Dogs thrive on routine, needing regular feeding schedules, exercise, and mental stimulation to stay healthy and happy. For busy city dwellers with demanding jobs or hectic schedules, finding the time to meet these needs can be a challenge.

Long hours spent at work or commuting can leave little time for quality interactions with a dog. Dogs are social creatures that crave companionship and attention, and extended periods of loneliness can lead to separation anxiety or destructive behaviors.

Owners must make arrangements for dog walkers, pet sitters, or daycare facilities to ensure their pets receive the care and attention they need during the day. This adds an additional financial burden and logistical challenge for owners who must coordinate schedules and ensure their furry friends are well-cared for in their absence.

Cost of Living

Urban living often comes with a higher cost of living, and this extends to pet ownership as well. The expenses associated with owning a dog in the city can add up quickly, including vet visits, grooming, food, and supplies. Additionally, some cities impose pet licensing fees or require specific vaccinations, adding to the financial considerations of urban dog ownership.

The cost of housing is also a significant factor to consider. Many pet-friendly apartments or condominiums charge additional pet deposits or monthly fees, increasing the overall housing expenses for dog owners. In competitive rental markets, finding affordable and pet-friendly housing can be a challenge, forcing some owners to make difficult choices between their living situation and their furry companions.

Despite these challenges, the rewards of urban dog ownership are abundant. The companionship, love, and happiness that dogs provide to their owners are beyond measure, enhancing the essence of urban communities and forging enduring connections between people and their beloved furry companions. By understanding and addressing the challenges of urban dog ownership, owners can create a fulfilling and harmonious life for themselves and their beloved pets amidst the bustling streets and towering skyscrapers of the cityscape.

Chapter 1
How is your Dog?

Small and Medium-Sized Dogs for Urban Living

As mentioned earlier, the bustling streets and compact living spaces of urban environments present unique challenges and opportunities for dog ownership. For those residing in apartments or houses with limited outdoor space, small and medium-sized breeds often make ideal companions. These dogs are well-suited to city life, offering a balance of energy, adaptability, and size that fits seamlessly into urban settings. Below, we explore a selection of small and medium-sized breeds known for their compatibility with urban living, highlighting their specific characteristics, behaviors, and their special bonds with humans.

French Bulldog

Size: Small

Temperament: Known for their affectionate and playful nature, French Bulldogs are excellent companions for urban dwellers. They have a calm demeanor, making them well-suited for apartment living.

Characteristics:

- Frenchies are sturdy dogs with a distinctive "bat-like" ear shape.
- They have a low exercise requirement, making short walks and indoor play sufficient to meet their needs.
- Their affectionate nature makes them loyal companions, often forming strong bonds with their owners.
- French Bulldogs are known for their adaptability to various living situations, whether it's a cozy apartment or a house with a small garden.

Relation with Humans:

- French Bulldogs are known to be excellent family dogs, often forming strong attachments to all members of the household.

- They are affectionate and thrive on human companionship, enjoying snuggling up with their owners on the couch.
- Due to their compact size, they are easy to transport, making them great travel companions for urban adventurers.
- Frenchies are also known for their comical antics, providing endless entertainment and laughter to their families.

Pug

Size: Small

Temperament: Pugs are charming, loving, and mischievous dogs, renowned for their playful and sociable nature. They adapt well to apartment living and are content with moderate exercise.

Characteristics:

- Pugs have a distinctive wrinkled face and a curled tail, giving them an endearing appearance.
- They are well-known for having personalities that are outgoing and friendly, which makes them wonderful companions for people as well as families.
- Pugs are relatively low-energy dogs, enjoying leisurely walks and indoor play sessions.
- They thrive on attention and are known to be "people dogs," seeking out human company at every opportunity.

Relation with Humans:

- Pugs are affectionate and devoted to their owners, often forming strong bonds with one person in particular.
- They are excellent with children and other pets, making them ideal family companions.
- Pugs have a knack for sensing their owners' moods and providing comfort when needed.
- Their playful nature makes them entertaining companions, always ready to engage in games and antics that bring joy to their households.

Cavalier King Charles Spaniel

Size: Small

Temperament: The Cavalier King Charles Spaniel is a gentle, affectionate, and graceful breed, well-suited to urban living. They are known for their friendly and sociable nature.

Characteristics:

- Cavaliers have a silky coat with distinctive feathering on the ears, chest, legs, and tail.
- They are adaptable dogs, equally content lounging indoors or exploring a small garden.
- Cavaliers have a moderate activity level, enjoying leisurely walks and interactive play sessions.
- They are intelligent and eager to please, making them relatively easy to train.

Relation with Humans:

- Cavaliers are loving and devoted companions, forming strong bonds with their families.
- They thrive on human interaction and do not do well when left alone for long periods.
- They are excellent with children and other pets, often assuming a gentle and patient demeanor.
- Cavaliers are known for their affectionate nature, enjoying snuggling up on laps or curling up beside their owners at night.

Boston Terrier

Size: Small

Temperament: Boston Terriers are friendly, intelligent, and lively dogs, well-suited to apartment living due to their compact size and moderate exercise needs.

Characteristics:

- Bostons have a tuxedo-like coat pattern, with a sleek and shiny coat.
- They are known for their expressive eyes and "smiling" faces, often conveying a sense of humor.
- Bostons are playful and energetic, enjoying interactive games and short walks around the neighborhood.
- They are relatively easy to train, responding well to positive reinforcement methods.

Relation with Humans:

- Boston Terriers are affectionate and loving companions, forming strong bonds with their families.
- They are known to be excellent with children, often assuming a protective and patient role.
- Bostons are sociable dogs, enjoying the company of both humans and other pets.
- They are adaptable to various living situations, thriving in apartments or houses with small yards.

Miniature Schnauzer

Size: Small to Medium

Temperament: Miniature Schnauzers are spirited, alert, and friendly dogs, known for their distinctive beards and eyebrows. They are adaptable to various living situations, making them well-suited for urban living.

Characteristics:

- Mini Schnauzers have a wiry coat that is often groomed in a "show cut" style.
- They are intelligent and eager to please, making them relatively easy to train.
- Schnauzers have a moderate energy level, enjoying brisk walks and interactive play sessions.
- They are known for their watchdog abilities, alerting their owners to any potential intruders.

Relation with Humans:

- Miniature Schnauzers are loyal and affectionate companions, forming strong bonds with their families.
- They are known to be excellent with children, often assuming a protective and playful role.
- Schnauzers are sociable dogs, enjoying the company of both humans and other pets.
- They have a tendency to be vocal, often "talking" to their owners through barks and grumbles, adding a touch of humor to daily interactions.

Shetland Sheepdog (Sheltie)

Size: Small to Medium

Temperament: The Shetland Sheepdog, or Sheltie, is an intelligent, energetic, and affectionate breed, well-suited to both apartment living and homes with small gardens.

Characteristics:

- Shelties have a striking coat with a luxurious mane and a plumed tail.
- They are highly intelligent and excel in obedience training and agility sports.
- Shelties have a moderate to high energy level, requiring regular exercise and mental stimulation.
- They are known for their herding instincts, often displaying a tendency to "herd" their family members.

Relation with Humans:

- Shetland Sheepdogs are loyal and devoted companions, forming deep bonds with their families.
- They are excellent with children, often assuming a protective and playful role.
- Shelties are sensitive dogs, attuned to their owners' emotions and moods.
- They thrive on companionship and do not do well when left alone for extended periods.

Bichon Frise

Size: Small

Temperament: The Bichon Frise is a cheerful, playful, and affectionate breed, known for its fluffy white coat and lively personality. They are well-suited to apartment living due to their small size and moderate exercise needs.

Characteristics:

- Bichons have a curly, hypoallergenic coat that requires regular grooming.
- They are playful and energetic, enjoying interactive games and short walks.
- Bichons are well-known for their outgoing and friendly personalities, which makes them wonderful companions for people as well as families.
- They are relatively adaptable to various living situations, thriving in apartments or houses with small yards.

Relation with Humans:

- Bichon Frises are loving and affectionate companions, forming strong bonds with their families.
- They are excellent with children, often assuming a playful and gentle demeanor.
- Bichons are sociable dogs, enjoying the company of both humans and other pets.
- They have a tendency to be clownish and entertaining, often eliciting laughter and smiles from their owners.

Cocker Spaniel

Size: Medium

Temperament: Cocker Spaniels are gentle, affectionate, and merry dogs, known for their silky coats and expressive eyes. They are well-suited to both apartment living and homes with small gardens.

Characteristics:

- Cockers have a luxurious, feathered coat that requires regular grooming.
- They are friendly and outgoing, often displaying a happy and wagging tail.
- Cockers have a moderate energy level, enjoying walks, hikes, and interactive play sessions.
- They are intelligent and eager to please, making them relatively easy to train.

Relation with Humans:

- Cocker Spaniels are loyal and devoted companions, forming strong bonds with their families.
- They are excellent with children, often assuming a gentle and patient role.
- Cockers are sociable dogs, enjoying the company of both humans and other pets.
- They are known for their affectionate nature, enjoying snuggling up on laps or curling up beside their owners at night.

Choosing the Right Breed for Your Urban Lifestyle

Selecting the perfect canine companion for urban living involves careful consideration of various factors, including your living situation, lifestyle, activity level, and preferences. Small and medium-sized dogs offer a fantastic array of options, each with its unique traits, temperaments, and requirements. Here, we delve into the essential aspects to consider when choosing the ideal breed to fit seamlessly into your urban lifestyle.

Energy Level

A crucial aspect to ponder when choosing a dog breed for urban living is its energy level. This characteristic typically dictates the breed's exercise requirements, playfulness, and overall activity level. Those with hectic schedules or limited outdoor space might find a dog with a lower energy level to be a more fitting choice.

For instance, breeds like the French Bulldog or Cavalier King Charles Spaniel have moderate energy levels, enjoying leisurely walks and indoor play sessions. These dogs are content with shorter bursts of activity, making them ideal for apartment living or smaller urban homes. On the other hand, breeds such as the Miniature Schnauzer or Sheltie have a higher energy level, requiring more vigorous exercise and mental stimulation to thrive.

Consider your own activity level and how much time you can dedicate to exercise and play. A dog's energy level should align with your lifestyle to ensure a harmonious and fulfilling companionship.

Space Requirements

Urban living often means limited indoor and outdoor space, especially in apartments or condos. When selecting a breed, consider its size and space requirements. Smaller breeds, such as the Pug or Boston Terrier, are well-suited for compact living spaces. They can comfortably curl up in cozy corners or find their favorite spot on the couch without taking up too much room.

For those with access to outdoor space, even if it's a small yard or nearby parks, breeds like the Miniature Schnauzer or Sheltie may thrive. These dogs enjoy the opportunity to stretch their legs and explore, making them a great fit for urban homes with a bit of green space nearby.

It's essential to ensure that your chosen breed can comfortably navigate and live within the confines of your urban dwelling. Consider factors such as access to outdoor areas for bathroom breaks, playtime, and exercise routines.

Temperament and Personality

Every breed has its unique temperament and personality traits, which play a significant role in their suitability for urban living. There are several breeds that are noted for their extroverted and social temperament, which makes them excellent companions for city adventures and interactions with both other dogs and people from the community.

For example, the friendly and playful Pug or Boston Terrier thrives in social settings, enjoying outings to dog parks, cafes, and city streets bustling with activity. These breeds are often eager to meet new people and make friends, adding a social element to your urban lifestyle.

Conversely, breeds such as the Cavalier King Charles Spaniel or Bichon Frise are renowned for their gentle and affectionate dispositions. They shine in offering emotional support and companionship, rendering them perfect for individuals or families in search of a loving and devoted companion in an urban setting.

When selecting a breed with a compatible temperament, it's essential to consider your own personality and lifestyle. Are you seeking a playful and outgoing companion to accompany you on city escapades, or do you lean towards a loyal and affectionate friend to curl up with after a bustling day? This introspection aids in finding the perfect match for a fulfilling companionship experience.

Grooming Needs

Another crucial aspect to consider when selecting a breed for urban living is its grooming requirements. While all dogs require some level of grooming, the extent can vary significantly between breeds. Some breeds have short, low-maintenance coats that require minimal grooming, ideal for those with busy schedules or limited time for grooming sessions.

Breeds like the French Bulldog or Boston Terrier have short coats that are relatively easy to maintain. Regular brushing to remove loose hair and occasional baths are usually sufficient to keep their coats healthy and shiny. These breeds are excellent choices for individuals or families looking for a low-maintenance grooming routine.

On the other hand, breeds such as the Cavalier King Charles Spaniel or Bichon Frise have longer, silky coats that require more attention. Regular brushing, grooming sessions, and occasional trims are necessary to prevent matting and maintain their coat's health and appearance. While these breeds may require more grooming care, the effort can be rewarding for those who enjoy the process and the bond it creates with their furry companion.

Consider your grooming preferences and capabilities when selecting a breed. Are you willing to invest time and effort into regular grooming sessions, or do you prefer a breed with minimal grooming needs?

Allergies and Shedding

For individuals or families with allergies, choosing a hypoallergenic breed or one with minimal shedding is essential. Breeds that produce less dander or shed less hair can be more suitable for those prone to allergies, allowing them to enjoy the companionship of a dog without triggering allergic reactions.

Hypoallergenic breeds, such as the Poodle, Bichon Frise, or Miniature Schnauzer, are often recommended for allergy sufferers. These breeds produce less dander and shed minimally, making them more compatible with individuals with allergies.

If allergies are a concern, consider breeds with hypoallergenic qualities or those that shed less hair. Keep in mind that regular grooming and cleaning routines can also help minimize allergens in the home.

Finding the Perfect Match

Choosing the right breed for your urban lifestyle is a deeply personal decision that involves considering your preferences, lifestyle, and living situation. It's essential to take the time to research and meet different breeds to find the perfect match for your needs and desires.

Begin by making a list of your priorities and requirements in a canine companion. Are you looking for a playful and outgoing breed that enjoys city adventures and social interactions? Or do you prefer a gentle and affectionate breed that provides emotional support and companionship?

Next, research breeds that align with your preferences, taking into account their energy levels, space requirements, grooming needs, and temperament. Online resources, breed-specific books, and reputable breeders or rescue organizations can provide valuable information about different breeds and their characteristics.

Once you have narrowed down your choices, consider meeting and interacting with dogs of those breeds. Visit local shelters, attend dog shows or events, or reach out to breeders or owners for introductions. Spending time with the dogs will give you a firsthand experience of their personalities, behaviors, and how they might fit into your life.

Before making a choice, you should not be afraid to inquire about the situation and ensure that you have as much information as feasible. Consider factors such as the breed's adaptability to city living, compatibility with your lifestyle, and the level of commitment required for their care.

Choosing the right breed for your urban lifestyle is an exciting and rewarding journey that culminates in the addition of a beloved companion to your life. Whether you opt for the playful antics of a Pug, the gentle loyalty of a Cavalier King Charles Spaniel, or the spirited energy of a Miniature Schnauzer, your furry friend will undoubtedly bring joy, companionship, and love to your urban adventures.

Remember that each breed has its unique qualities, traits, and needs. Take the time to consider what you are looking for in a canine companion and how your chosen breed will fit into your lifestyle and living situation.

Understanding Canine Intelligence

Canine intelligence is a fascinating subject, and dogs exhibit various types of intelligence that contribute to their problem-solving abilities, learning capacity, and overall cognitive skills. While it's important to note that intelligence can vary among individual dogs, researchers have identified different types of canine intelligence based on their specific strengths and abilities.

Instinctive Intelligence

Instinctive intelligence refers to a dog's natural abilities and instincts that are inherited from their breed or ancestral lineage. Different breeds have been selectively bred for specific purposes, such as herding, hunting, guarding, or retrieving. Dogs with high instinctive intelligence excel in tasks related to their breed's original purpose. For example, herding breeds like Border Collies have a strong instinct for herding and exhibit exceptional problem-solving skills when it comes to controlling and guiding livestock.

Adaptive Intelligence

Adaptive intelligence refers to a dog's ability to learn from and adapt to new situations or environments. Dogs with high adaptive intelligence can quickly understand and adjust their behavior to changing circumstances. They possess excellent problem-solving skills and can apply their past experiences to novel situations. This type of intelligence is often observed in working and service dog breeds, as they need to adapt to various tasks and environments to fulfill their roles effectively.

Obedience Intelligence

Obedience intelligence refers to a dog's ability to understand and follow commands or cues from their human handlers. Dogs with high obedience intelligence are quick to learn and exhibit a strong desire to please their owners. They are attentive, responsive, and can master a wide range of commands and tasks. Breeds like Border Collies, German Shepherds, and Golden Retrievers often excel in obedience training and can perform complex tasks with precision and reliability.

Problem-Solving Intelligence

Problem-solving intelligence refers to a dog's ability to analyze and solve problems. Dogs with high problem-solving intelligence exhibit advanced cognitive skills and can figure out solutions to challenges or puzzles. They demonstrate excellent observational skills, logical thinking, and the ability to overcome obstacles. This type of intelligence is often observed in breeds like Poodles, Australian Shepherds, and Rottweilers, who excel in activities that require problem-solving, such as agility courses or interactive puzzle toys.

Social Intelligence

Social intelligence refers to a dog's ability to understand and interact effectively with other animals, including humans and fellow dogs. Dogs with high social intelligence demonstrate excellent communication skills, empathy, and the ability to read social cues. They can understand human emotions and respond accordingly. Breeds like Labrador Retrievers, Cavalier King Charles Spaniels, and Boxers are known for their high social intelligence, making them great therapy or assistance dogs.

Sensory Intelligence

Sensory intelligence refers to a dog's heightened senses and their ability to interpret and respond to sensory information. Dogs have a superior sense of smell, hearing, and vision compared to humans, and breeds that excel in sensory intelligence have a heightened sensitivity to their environment. For instance, Bloodhounds have an exceptional sense of smell and are often used in tracking and search operations due to their ability to detect and follow scents. Sight hounds like Greyhounds have remarkable visual acuity and speed, allowing them to excel in activities like lure coursing.

It's important to recognize that these different types of intelligence are not mutually exclusive, and many dogs exhibit a combination of these qualities. Additionally, individual dogs within a breed may vary in their strengths and aptitudes.

Assessing Your Dog's Strengths and Weaknesses

Understanding your dog's unique abilities, preferences, and areas that may need improvement is a crucial part of assessing their strengths and weaknesses. This knowledge enables you to tailor your approach to their training and provide the necessary support. By identifying their strengths, you can capitalize on their talents and provide suitable outlets for them to thrive. Conversely, recognizing weaknesses allows you to address them through targeted training and offer additional assistance as required. In this section, we will delve into the process of assessing your dog's strengths and weaknesses and explore how you can utilize this understanding to enhance their overall well-being.

Observation and Interaction

The first step in assessing your dog's strengths and weaknesses is to spend quality time observing and interacting with them. Observe their behavior, reactions, and responses in various situations and environments. Note their preferred activities, interactions with other dogs or humans, and any particular behaviors or skills that stand out.

Pay attention to the following areas:

- Physical Abilities: Observe your dog's physical capabilities, such as speed, agility, endurance, and coordination. Note if they excel in activities that require physical strength or have any limitations or difficulties in specific movements.

- Temperament and Personality: Assess your dog's temperament and personality traits. Are they outgoing and confident or more reserved and cautious? Do they adapt well to new situations, or do they tend to be anxious or fearful? Understanding their temperament helps determine the best approach to training and socialization.

- Communication Skills: Observe how well your dog communicates with you and other dogs or animals. Do they understand and respond to verbal commands or body language cues? Are they good at expressing their needs or emotions? Communication skills play a crucial role in training and overall well-being.

- Social Interactions: Assess how your dog interacts with other dogs, animals, and humans. Do they enjoy socializing and playing with other dogs? Are they comfortable around new people or do they display signs of fear or aggression? Understanding their social interactions helps create a safe and positive environment for them.

Training and Skill Assessment

Training and skill assessment involve evaluating your dog's abilities in specific areas and identifying areas that may require further training or improvement. This assessment can help you tailor training programs to focus on their strengths and work on any weaknesses. Consider the following factors:

- Obedience and Basic Commands: Assess how well your dog responds to basic commands such as sit, stay, come, and heel. Determine their level of obedience and their understanding of commands. This assessment will help you gauge their level of training and identify areas that may need reinforcement.

- Specific Skills: Evaluate your dog's skills in activities specific to their breed or desired activities. For example, if you have a retriever, assess their retrieving skills and their ability to follow scent trails. If you have a herding breed, observe their herding instincts and their ability to respond to herding commands. This assessment will help you identify areas of natural talent and potential areas for further development.

- Problem-Solving Abilities: Assess your dog's problem-solving abilities by introducing them to puzzles or interactive toys. Observe how they approach challenges and if they can figure out solutions. This assessment can give you insight into their cognitive abilities and their capacity for problem-solving.

- Behavioral Issues: Identify any behavioral issues or challenges your dog may have, such as excessive barking, separation anxiety, or fear-based reactions. Understanding these issues helps you address them through training, behavior modification techniques, or seeking professional help if needed.

Seeking Professional Guidance

In some cases, seeking professional guidance from a dog trainer, behaviorist, or veterinarian may be beneficial, especially when dealing with complex behavioral issues or specialized training requirements. A professional can provide an objective assessment of your dog's strengths and weaknesses and offer guidance on how to address specific areas of concern.

Working with Your Dog's Strengths and Weaknesses

Once you have assessed your dog's strengths and weaknesses, you can create a plan to work with them effectively. Here are some strategies to consider:

1. **Capitalize on Strengths:** Provide opportunities for your dog to engage in activities that align with their strengths. If they excel in physical activities, consider participating in agility or obedience trials. If they have strong problem-solving abilities, provide them with interactive toys or engage them in puzzle-solving games. By capitalizing on their strengths, you can provide outlets for their talents and keep them mentally and physically stimulated.

2. **Address Weaknesses through Training:** For areas where your dog may have weaknesses, such as obedience or socialization, focus on targeted training. When training your dog, it's helpful to break down tasks into small, manageable steps. This approach makes learning easier and more achievable for your canine companion. Additionally, employing positive reinforcement techniques—such as offering treats, praise, or playtime—can encourage progress and reinforce desired behaviors. For complex behavioral issues or if you're facing challenges in training, don't hesitate to seek professional help. Professional dog trainers or behaviorists can provide valuable guidance, personalized strategies, and expertise to address specific issues effectively.

3. **Provide Mental Stimulation:** Regardless of their strengths and weaknesses, all dogs benefit from mental stimulation. Incorporate activities that engage their minds, such as interactive toys, puzzle games, scent work, or obedience training sessions. Mental stimulation helps prevent boredom, strengthens their cognitive abilities, and contributes to their overall well-being.

4. **Practice Positive Reinforcement:** Positive reinforcement is a powerful tool in training and building a strong bond with your dog. Reward their successes, no matter how small, with treats, praise, or playtime. Positive reinforcement encourages desired behaviors, boosts their confidence, and fosters a positive learning environment.

5. **Be Patient and Understanding:** Every dog is unique, and progress may vary. Be patient with your dog as they learn and grow. Understand their limitations and provide a supportive and nurturing environment. Celebrate their successes and be understanding when they face challenges or setbacks.

Assessing your dog's strengths and weaknesses is an ongoing process. As they grow, learn, and experience new things, their abilities may change or develop further. Regularly reassess their skills, observe their behavior, and adapt your training and activities accordingly.

Tailoring Exercises to Stimulate Specific Intelligence Areas

By identifying your dog's specific intelligence strengths and weaknesses, you can design activities that target and develop specific intelligence areas. Here, we provide examples of exercises to stimulate each intelligence area.

Instinctive Intelligence

To stimulate instinctive intelligence, provide activities that tap into their breed's inherent skills. Here are some examples:

- Herding Breeds: Set up a mini-obstacle course using cones or other objects and guide your dog through it using commands such as "come by" or "away to me." You can also introduce them to herding balls or frisbees to encourage their herding instincts.

- Retrieving Breeds: Engage your dog in retrieving games, using toys or balls. Start with short distances and gradually increase the distance. Incorporate commands like "fetch" or "drop it" to enhance their retrieving skills.

- Scent Hounds: Hide treats or toys in your backyard or a designated area and encourage your dog to use their exceptional sense of smell to locate them. An other option is to present them with tasks that involve smell work, in which they are required to seek for particular odors or things.

Adaptive Intelligence

To stimulate adaptive intelligence, provide activities that challenge their problem-solving abilities and encourage learning. Here are some examples:

- Puzzle Toys: Consider investing in interactive puzzle toys that engage your dog's cognitive abilities by requiring them to solve challenges to access treats or hidden compartments. Begin with simpler puzzles and gradually escalate the difficulty level as your dog becomes more adept at solving them.

- Hide and Seek: Teach your dog to look for goodies or toys that you have hidden in various places about your home or yard, and then reward him or her for finding them. Increase the complexity by hiding them in more challenging spots or using scent cues to guide them.

- Training Variations: Vary your training routines and introduce new commands or tricks regularly. This keeps your dog engaged and encourages them to think and adapt to new tasks.

Obedience Intelligence

To stimulate obedience intelligence, focus on training exercises that strengthen their responsiveness and reliability. Here are some examples:

- Basic Commands: Practice basic commands such as sit, stay, come, and heel in different environments and with increasing distractions. This helps your dog generalize the commands and respond reliably in various situations.
- Advanced Training: Teach your dog advanced commands or tricks like "roll over," "play dead," or "find it." These exercises challenge their obedience intelligence and enhance their learning capacity.
- Canine Sports: Engage your dog in activities like agility, rally obedience, or obedience competitions. These sports require precise obedience and help sharpen their responsiveness to commands.

Problem-Solving Intelligence

To stimulate problem-solving intelligence, provide activities that require critical thinking and problem-solving skills. Here are some examples:

- Interactive Toys: Use toys that require your dog to solve puzzles to access treats or toys. These toys may have hidden compartments, sliding panels, or multiple layers that your dog needs to navigate.
- Treat Dispensing Games: Hide treats in a muffin tin covered with tennis balls. Your dog will have to remove the balls to access the treats. This exercise encourages them to use their problem-solving skills to get their rewards.
- Shape and Color Discrimination: Teach your dog to recognize and differentiate between shapes or colors. Start with simple exercises like matching toys to their corresponding shapes or colors and gradually increase the complexity.

Social Intelligence

To stimulate social intelligence, engage your dog in activities that promote positive social interactions. Here are some examples:

- Playdates: Arrange playdates with other friendly and well-socialized dogs. This allows your dog to practice their social skills, including proper play behavior, sharing toys, and reading social cues from other dogs.
- Group Training Classes: Enroll your dog in group training classes where they can interact with other dogs and their owners under the guidance of a professional trainer. This provides a controlled and structured environment for socialization.
- Therapy Dog Programs: If your dog has a calm and friendly temperament, consider getting them certified as a therapy dog. This allows them to interact with different people in various settings, providing valuable socialization opportunities.

Sensory Intelligence

To stimulate sensory intelligence, engage your dog in activities that focus on their senses. Here are some examples:

- Scent Work: Introduce your dog to scent work activities, where they have to search for specific scents or objects. Begin your dog's training with straightforward exercises and gradually escalate both the complexity and difficulty level over time.

- Sound Recognition: Play different sounds, such as doorbells, sirens, or animal noises, and associate them with specific actions or commands. This helps your dog recognize and respond to different sounds.

- Visual Stimulation: Provide visual stimulation by showing your dog videos or movies featuring animals or nature scenes. This can captivate their attention and engage their visual senses.

Chapter 2
How to Make your Dog Play

Engaging in playtime with our canine companions is not just a delightful pastime—it's a fundamental aspect of their well-being and cognitive development. This interactive and lively interaction offers a plethora of benefits for dogs, encompassing both physical and mental facets.

Physical Benefits of Playtime

First and foremost, play serves as a natural avenue for dogs to expend their energy, exercise their bodies, and maintain optimal physical fitness. During play, dogs indulge in a range of movements, including running, jumping, fetching, and wrestling. These activities promote cardiovascular health, muscle development, and overall agility. Regular play sessions play a pivotal role in preventing obesity, improving coordination, and enhancing their overall physical condition.

Additionally, the physical activity during play releases endorphins, often referred to as the "feel-good" hormones. These endorphins not only promote relaxation and reduce stress but also contribute to a positive emotional state. It's akin to witnessing the joyous sprint of a dog chasing a ball or the exuberant leaps during a game of fetch—all contributing to a healthier, happier pup.

Social Interaction and Development

Playtime serves as a vital avenue for social interaction for our canine friends. Dogs, being inherently social animals, benefit greatly from these playful interactions. Whether it's romping with fellow canines, engaging in a game of tug-of-war with humans, or simply exploring with other species, play helps dogs develop crucial social skills.

Through these interactions, dogs learn vital lessons such as bite inhibition, appropriate play behaviors, and understanding social cues. They refine their communication skills, establish bonds with others, and foster a sense of belonging within their social groups. This socialization during play significantly contributes to their mental and emotional well-being.

Cognitive Development Through Play

Beyond the physical and social aspects, playtime also plays a pivotal role in a dog's cognitive development. Dogs are intelligent creatures, blessed with curiosity and problem-solving abilities. Engaging in play stimulates their minds, enhances mental agility, and boosts cognitive functions.

Let's delve into some specific ways in which play contributes to a dog's cognitive development:

• Problem-Solving Skills

Certain play activities, such as puzzle toys or interactive games, present dogs with challenges that require problem-solving abilities. These mental puzzles encourage critical thinking, creativity, and the development of innovative solutions. Watching a dog navigate a treat-dispensing toy or figure out a challenging puzzle brings to light their impressive problem-solving prowess.

• Focus and Concentration

Play sessions that involve training games or activities requiring dogs to follow instructions sharpen their focus and concentration. Dogs learn to pay attention, listen for cues, and respond appropriately. This honing of their cognitive abilities enhances their overall trainability and responsiveness.

• Memory and Learning

Engaging in playtime that involves learning new tricks or commands enhances a dog's memory and learning skills. Dogs remember cues, associate them with specific actions, and retain knowledge gained through play. It's a delightful sight to see a dog recall a trick learned during a playful training session.

• Sensory Stimulation

Play engages a dog's senses—sight, smell, hearing, and touch. Different toys, textures, and environments stimulate their sensory perception, enriching their cognitive abilities. Whether it's the excitement of chasing a squeaky toy or exploring different scents during a game of hide-and-seek, these sensory experiences contribute to their cognitive development.

• Emotional Intelligence

Playtime also plays a pivotal role in developing a dog's emotional intelligence. Through play, dogs learn to interpret and respond to various emotional cues, both from humans and fellow canines. This understanding of emotions fosters empathy, enhances their ability to form social bonds, and contributes to their emotional well-being.

The Essential Guide to Carefree Playtime with Your Canine Companion

Communication between dogs and humans may seem like a conversation in different languages, but when it comes to playing together, a beautiful form of understanding can unfold. To ensure that playtime is an absolute delight for both you and your four-legged friend, there are some fundamental rules to follow.

Relaxation is Key

To set the stage for carefree play, the first rule is to loosen up. When calling your dog over, get down on your knees to their level. Use not just your voice but also your hands to communicate. Take a few steps forward, then pause. The goal here is to entice your dog to chase after you. This subtle invitation signals to your furry companion that it's time for fun and games to begin.

Mastering Your Voice

The next foundational exercise revolves around your voice. Remember that volume isn't crucial, as dogs hear significantly better than humans do. You can lower your volume slightly without any issues. What matters most is the tone—always keep it friendly and upbeat. Just like with people, a positive mood is contagious. Practice praising, as it can be nearly as rewarding for your dog as a treat.

Rewards Galore

When it comes to rewards, you have a range of options to choose from. These can include gentle caresses, enthusiastic praise, tasty treats, or even your dog's favorite toy or game. Naturally, treats often serve as the strongest incentive for your four-legged friend. During the training phase, it's perfectly fine to reward your dog for every successful step. However, gradually transition to a less frequent reward system. It's crucial to avoid overindulgence with treats to prevent weight gain. Everything should be done in moderation and with a clear purpose.

Frequent praise and strokes also serve as excellent rewards. Your dog will bask in the joy of your affection, and there's no need to hold back on those heartfelt expressions of approval.

Timing is Everything

For the perfect playtime experience, always keep this in mind: your dog lives in the present moment. To ensure that a reward truly resonates, deliver it at the right moment. Wait for up to a second before offering praise or a treat. This allows your dog to savor the joy of playing and solidify what it has learned. Additionally, it's beneficial to teach your dog a signal for stopping, even in the midst of play.

You're the Leader

Even amidst the joyous chaos of play, remember that you are the boss. This awareness is crucial. It instills a sense of security in your dog, benefiting both of you immensely. You set the rules, determine when playtime commences, and decide what tricks to teach and rewards to give. Being the leader also fosters a healthy dynamic, ensuring a harmonious and enjoyable play experience.

In the enchanting world of playtime with your canine companion, these fundamental rules serve as guiding lights. Embrace relaxation, master the art of your voice, select rewards wisely, perfect your timing, and maintain your role as the leader. With these principles in mind, every play session becomes a joyous and enriching experience for you and your beloved dog.

Playing with your dog isn't just about fun and games—it's a vital aspect of their overall well-being and happiness. From boosting physical fitness to enhancing mental stimulation, engaging in various play activities strengthens the bond between you and your furry companion. To ensure your dog stays active and entertained, here are some exciting and interactive games to try:

Food Games

Incorporating food into playtime engages a dog's sense of smell, taste, and problem-solving abilities. Dogs have a natural inclination to seek out food, making food-related games both stimulating and rewarding. These activities tap into their primal instincts, providing mental challenges as they work to access their treats. Food games also encourage slower eating, reducing the risk of digestive issues and promoting a healthy relationship with food.

Treat Dispensing Toys

Treat Dispensing Toys provide mental stimulation and combat boredom by requiring your dog to work for their treats. These toys come in various forms, such as puzzle feeders or Kong toys, and challenge your dog to manipulate them to release hidden rewards.

- *How many persons can be involved:* This game is best suited for solo play between you and your dog, as it involves the dog working independently with the toy.
- *Can it be played by a child alone:* While adult supervision is recommended, an older child can participate in this game, filling the toy with treats and observing the dog's interaction.
- *What you'll need:* Treat-dispensing toys like puzzle feeders or Kong toys, and your dog's favorite treats or kibble.

Instructions:

1. Fill the treat-dispensing toy with your dog's favorite treats or kibble.
2. Demonstrate how the toy works by manipulating it to release the treats.
3. Encourage your dog to interact with the toy and figure out how to extract the treats.
4. Offer verbal praise and rewards when they successfully retrieve the treats from the toy.

Hide-and-Seek Treats

Hide-and-Seek Treats is a fantastic game that taps into your dog's inherent scavenging instincts. This interactive activity encourages your dog to use their sense of smell and problem-solving abilities to locate hidden treats around your home or yard.

- *How many persons can be involved:* While this game is primarily designed for solo play between you and your dog, it can also involve multiple family members who take turns hiding treats.
- *Can it be played by a child alone:* Yes, a child can participate in this game independently under adult supervision, ensuring that the treats are hidden in safe and accessible locations.
- *What you'll need:* Your dog's favorite treats and some designated hiding spots.

Instructions:

1. Show your dog a treat to capture their interest.
2. While your dog observes, hide the treat in a specific location.
3. Encourage your dog to find the treat using verbal cues like "Find it!" or "Search!"
4. Celebrate their success by praising them and offering additional treats or a pat on the head.

Find the Treats in a Box

Find the Treats in a Box is a stimulating game that challenges your dog's searching skills as they rummage through crumpled paper to uncover hidden treats.

- *How many persons can be involved:* This game is best suited for solo play between you and your dog.
- *Can it be played by a child alone:* Yes, under adult supervision, a child can set up the game and observe the dog's interaction.
- *What you'll need:* A cardboard box, crumpled paper, and treats.

Instructions:

1. Place treats inside the cardboard box and cover them with crumpled paper.
2. Allow your dog to use their nose and paws to dig through the paper and find the hidden treats.
3. Celebrate their success by praising them and offering additional treats or affection.

Snuffle Mat Game

The Snuffle Mat Game engages your dog's sense of smell and provides mental stimulation as they search for treats hidden within a mat filled with fabric strips.

- *How many persons can be involved:* This game is ideally designed for solo play between you and your dog, but multiple family members can participate in creating a more challenging setup.
- *Can it be played by a child alone:* Yes, under adult supervision, a child can set up the game and encourage the dog to find treats within the mat.
- *What you'll need:* A snuffle mat or a towel and your dog's treats or kibble.

Instructions:

1. Sprinkle your dog's treats or kibble onto the snuffle mat or towel, ensuring they are hidden within the fabric strips.
2. Encourage your dog to use their nose to search and sniff out the treats.
3. Celebrate their success as they find each hidden treat by praising them and offering additional treats or affection.

Muffin Tin Game

The Muffin Tin Game challenges your dog's problem-solving skills as they uncover hidden treats placed in a muffin tin.

- *How many persons can be involved:* This game is best suited for solo play, but multiple family members can participate in setting up the game or supervising.
- *Can it be played by a child alone:* Yes, under adult supervision, a child can place treats in the muffin tin cups.
- *What you'll need:* A muffin tin, some tennis balls or plastic cups, and your dog's favorite treats.

Instructions:

1. Place treats in some of the muffin tin cups.
2. Cover each cup with a tennis ball or plastic cup to create a hiding spot.
3. Encourage your dog to find the treats by sniffing and removing the covering objects.
4. Reward your dog with praise and additional treats when they successfully uncover the treats.

Cupcake Tin Game

The Cupcake Tin Game adds a creative twist to traditional treat-hunting activities by using a cupcake tin to hide treats for your dog to find.

- *How many persons can be involved:* While designed for solo play, multiple family members can join in the setup or observe the game.
- *Can it be played by a child alone:* Yes, under adult supervision, a child can place treats in the cupcake tin cups.
- *What you'll need:* A cupcake tin, small treats, and covering items like crumpled paper or toys.

Instructions:

1. Place a treat in each cup of the cupcake tin.
2. Cover each cup with a small ball of crumpled paper or a toy.
3. Encourage your dog to uncover the treats by removing the covers.
4. Reward your dog with praise and treats each time they reveal a tasty surprise.

Treat Toss and Fetch

Treat Toss and Fetch combines the excitement of fetch with the gratification of treats, encouraging your dog to chase and retrieve a toy while enjoying a tasty reward.

- *How many persons can be involved:* This game is ideally suited for solo play between you and your dog.
- *Can it be played by a child alone:* Yes, under adult supervision, a child can participate in tossing the toy and observing the dog's retrieves.
- *What you'll need:* Your dog's favorite treats and a suitable toy for fetching.

Instructions:

1. Show your dog the toy and let them become interested in it.
2. Toss the toy a short distance, encouraging your dog to chase after it.
3. When your dog retrieves the toy, reward them with praise and a treat.
4. Repeat the game, gradually increasing the distance of the throws and continuing to reward your dog for successful retrieves.

Snack Stash Game

The Snack Stash Game challenges your dog to search for hidden treats placed in various locations around your home, providing mental stimulation and a rewarding scavenger hunt experience.

- *How many persons can be involved:* This game is ideally suited for solo play between you and your dog.
- *Can it be played by a child alone:* Yes, under adult supervision, a child can hide treats and observe the dog's search.
- *What you'll need:* Your dog's favorite treats and different hiding spots around your home.

Instructions:

1. Hide treats in various locations around your home, such as under pillows, behind doors, or inside shoeboxes.
2. Encourage your dog to search for the hidden treats using verbal cues like "Find it!" or "Search!"
3. Celebrate their success each time they discover a hidden treat by praising them and offering additional treats or affection.

Tug-of-War with Treat Rope

Tug-of-War with Treat Rope combines the excitement of play with the gratification of rewards by integrating treats into a classic game of tug-of-war.

- *How many persons can be involved:* This game is ideally suited for one-on-one interaction between you and your dog.
- *Can it be played by a child alone:* While adult supervision is recommended, a child can participate in this game, provided they understand how to engage safely with the dog.
- *What you'll need:* A sturdy rope and small treats.

Instructions:

1. Tie small treats at intervals along the length of the rope.
2. Engage in a game of tug-of-war with your dog, allowing them to grab and enjoy the treats as they pull on the rope.
3. Use positive reinforcement by praising your dog during play and offering additional treats or rewards for their efforts.

Bobbing for Treats

Bobbing for Treats introduces a fun water-based challenge where your dog retrieves treats from a water-filled container, adding excitement and physical activity to their playtime.

- *How many persons can be involved:* This game is best suited for solo play between you and your dog.
- *Can it be played by a child alone:* Yes, under adult supervision, a child can participate in setting up the game and observing the dog's interaction with the water.
- *What you'll need:* A large bucket or basin filled with water and floating treats.

Instructions:

1. Place the floating treats in the water-filled bucket or basin.
2. Encourage your dog to use their snout or mouth to retrieve the treats from the water.
3. Monitor them closely to ensure their safety and offer positive reinforcement for their efforts.

Hunting Games

Hunting games allow dogs to channel their inner hunter, satisfying their instinctual drive to chase and catch prey. These activities stimulate their senses of sight, smell, and hearing, providing mental and physical exercise. By hiding toys or treats for them to find, dogs engage in a rewarding and fulfilling task that mimics their natural behaviors in the wild. Hunting games also promote problem-solving skills and boost their confidence as they successfully locate their "prey."

Treasure Hunt

The Treasure Hunt game challenges your dog's tracking skills as they search for hidden treats or toys, turning their playtime into an exciting quest.

- *How many persons can be involved:* This game is best suited for solo play between you and your dog.
- *Can it be played by a child alone:* Yes, under adult supervision, a child can hide treats or toys and observe the dog's search.
- *What you'll need:* Small treats or toys and various hiding spots.

Instructions:

1. Hide small treats or toys in different locations around your home or yard.
2. Encourage your dog to search for the hidden treasures by using verbal cues like "Find it!" or "Search!"
3. Celebrate their success each time they find a hidden treasure by praising them and offering additional treats or playtime with the toy.

Retrieve and Fetch

The Retrieve and Fetch game taps into your dog's natural retrieving instincts, turning a simple game of fetch into a rewarding and interactive experience.

- *How many persons can be involved:* This game is ideally suited for one-on-one interaction between you and your dog.
- *Can it be played by a child alone:* Yes, under adult supervision, a child can participate in tossing the toy and observing the dog's retrieves.
- *What you'll need:* A toy suitable for fetching.

Instructions:

1. Show your dog the toy and let them become interested in it.
2. Toss the toy a short distance, encouraging your dog to chase after it.
3. When your dog retrieves the toy, celebrate their success and encourage them to bring it back to you.
4. Reward your dog with praise and playtime with the toy after each successful retrieve.

Flirt Pole

The Flirt Pole game mimics prey-like movements, activating your dog's natural hunting instincts and providing a physical and mental challenge.

- *How many persons can be involved:* This game is best suited for solo play between you and your dog.
- *Can it be played by a child alone:* Yes, under adult supervision, a child can manipulate the flirt pole and observe the dog's reactions.
- *What you'll need:* A flirt pole (a long pole with a rope or toy attached).

Instructions:

1. Move the flirt pole in a way that mimics the movements of prey, such as quick jerks and sudden stops.
2. Encourage your dog to chase and catch the toy attached to the flirt pole.
3. Allow your dog to "win" by capturing the toy periodically to keep them engaged and satisfied.
4. Reward your dog with praise and playtime after each successful capture.

Find the Hidden Toy

The Find the Hidden Toy game engages your dog's sense of smell as they embark on a mission to discover a concealed toy.

- *How many persons can be involved:* This game is designed for one-on-one interaction between you and your dog.
- *Can it be played by a child alone:* Yes, under adult supervision, a child can participate in hiding the toy and observing the dog's search.
- *What you'll need:* Your dog's favorite toy and various hiding spots.

Instructions:

1. Show your dog the toy to spark their interest.
2. While your dog watches, hide the toy in a specific location.
3. Encourage your dog to find the toy using verbal cues like "Find it!" or "Search!"
4. Celebrate their success when they discover the hidden toy by praising them and engaging in a playful interaction with the toy.

Freeze and Find

The Freeze and Find game adds a dynamic challenge to traditional hide and seek by having your dog locate you when you freeze in different positions.

- *How many persons can be involved:* This game is best played solo or with one additional person to help with positioning.
- *Can it be played by a child alone:* Under adult supervision, a child can participate in the freeze positions and observe the dog's search.
- *What you'll need:* Treats and a willingness to freeze in various positions.

Instructions:

1. Start with a simple freeze position, such as standing still with your arms crossed.
2. Ask your dog to stay or have someone hold them.
3. Freeze in the chosen position and call your dog's name or use a cue phrase like "Find me!"
4. Encourage your dog to search for you and give them hints or cues if needed.
5. Celebrate their success when they find you by praising them and offering treats as a reward.

Lure and Chase

The Lure and Chase game imitates the movements of prey, fostering your dog's natural instinct to chase and capture a lure toy.

- *How many persons can be involved:* This game is designed for solo play between you and your dog.
- *Can it be played by a child alone:* Yes, under adult supervision, a child can manipulate the lure toy and observe the dog's reactions.
- *What you'll need:* A lure toy (such as a flirt pole or feather wand).

Instructions:

1. Move the lure toy in a way that mimics the movements of prey, such as quick dashes and sudden changes in direction.
2. Encourage your dog to chase and capture the lure toy.
3. Allow your dog to "win" by catching the toy periodically to keep them engaged and satisfied.
4. Reward your dog with praise and playtime after each successful capture.

Balloon Hunt

The Balloon Hunt game adds an element of excitement by engaging your dog's hunting instincts, requiring them to pop balloons to reveal hidden treats or toys.

- *How many persons can be involved:* This game is best suited for solo play between you and your dog.
- *Can it be played by a child alone:* Yes, under adult supervision, a child can inflate balloons, insert treats or toys, and observe the dog's interaction.
- *What you'll need:* Balloons, treats or toys, and a pin or sharp object for popping the balloons.

Instructions:

1. Insert treats or toys into the uninflated balloons.
2. Inflate the balloons and scatter them around an enclosed area.
3. Encourage your dog to chase and pop the balloons to access the hidden treats or toys.
4. Celebrate their success by praising them and offering additional rewards.

Feather Chase

The Feather Chase game mimics prey-like movements, engaging your dog's hunting instincts through interactive play with a feather wand or fishing pole toy.

- *How many persons can be involved:* This game is best suited for solo play between you and your dog.
- *Can it be played by a child alone:* Yes, under adult supervision, a child can manipulate the feather wand or fishing pole toy and observe the dog's reactions.
- *What you'll need:* A feather wand or fishing pole toy with feathers attached.

Instructions:

1. Move the feather wand or fishing pole toy in a way that mimics the movements of prey, such as quick darting motions.
2. Encourage your dog to chase and capture the feathers.
3. Allow your dog to "win" by catching the feathers periodically to keep them engaged and satisfied.
4. Reward your dog with praise and playtime after each successful capture.

Digging for Treasure

The Digging for Treasure game allows your dog to express their natural digging instincts while uncovering hidden treats or toys in a designated digging area.

- *How many persons can be involved:* This game is designed for solo play between you and your dog.
- *Can it be played by a child alone:* Yes, under adult supervision, a child can participate in setting up the digging area and observing the dog's engagement.
- *What you'll need:* A designated digging area (such as a sandbox) and treats or toys.

Instructions:

1. Bury treats or toys in the designated digging area.
2. Encourage your dog to dig and search for the buried treasures.
3. Celebrate their success when they uncover the hidden treats or toys by praising them and offering additional rewards.

Laser Pointer

The Laser Pointer game stimulates your dog's chase instinct as they attempt to catch the elusive light.

- *How many persons can be involved:* This game is designed for solo play between you and your dog.

- *Can it be played by a child alone:* Yes, under adult supervision, a child can handle the laser pointer and observe the dog's reactions.

- *What you'll need:* A laser pointer.

Instructions:

1. Shine the laser pointer on the ground or walls in a way that mimics the movement of prey.
2. Encourage your dog to chase and follow the light.
3. Occasionally redirect the laser to a treat or toy, allowing your dog to "capture" the reward.
4. Reward your dog with praise and playtime after each session.

Scent Games

Dogs possess an incredible sense of smell, and scent games harness this ability for stimulating play. By introducing scents for dogs to identify or hiding treats based on scent cues, these activities engage their olfactory senses. Scent games provide mental stimulation and encourage dogs to use their noses in creative ways. They also offer a sense of accomplishment as dogs successfully track down hidden scents, boosting their confidence and mental well-being.

Scent Trails

The Scent Trails game taps into your dog's natural tracking instincts, allowing them to follow a specific scent trail to discover hidden treats or toys.

- *How many persons can be involved:* This game is best played solo or with one person guiding the dog along the scent trail.
- *Can it be played by a child alone:* Under adult supervision, a child can participate in setting up the scent trail and observing the dog's engagement.
- *What you'll need:* Treats or toys, a long leash or rope, and a scent trail (e.g., treats crushed and scattered along a path).

Instructions:

1. Create a scent trail by scattering crushed treats along a specific path or using a scent drag (a cloth with scent on it).
2. Attach your dog to a long leash or rope.
3. Walk along the scent trail, allowing your dog to follow the scent and find the hidden treats or toys.
4. Celebrate their success when they reach the end of the trail by praising them and offering rewards.

Scent Recognition

The Scent Recognition game is a stimulating activity that enhances your dog's ability to identify and distinguish various scents.

- *How many persons can be involved:* This game is best played solo or with one person to guide the activity.
- *Can it be played by a child alone:* Under adult supervision, a child can participate in presenting scented items and observing the dog's response.
- *What you'll need:* Different scented items, such as cotton balls infused with various essential oils or food extracts.

Instructions:

1. Introduce your dog to each scented item, allowing them to sniff and become familiar with the scent.
2. Present two or more scented items and ask your dog to touch or indicate the specific scent you're cueing.
3. Reward your dog with praise and treats when they correctly identify the target scent.

Scent Discrimination

The Scent Discrimination game challenges your dog to distinguish and locate specific scents among a variety of objects.

- *How many persons can be involved:* This game is best played solo or with one person guiding the activity.
- *Can it be played by a child alone:* Under adult supervision, a child can participate in arranging objects and observing the dog's response.
- *What you'll need:* Different objects (e.g., cups, boxes, or containers) and scented items (e.g., cotton balls with different scents).

Instructions:

1. Place a scented item, such as a cotton ball infused with a specific scent, inside one of the objects.
2. Arrange the objects in a row or spread them out.
3. Encourage your dog to use their nose to find the object with the matching scent.
4. Celebrate their success when they identify the correct object by praising them and offering rewards.

Scented Muffin Tin

The Scented Muffin Tin game challenges your dog's olfactory abilities as they seek out treats hidden under cups in a muffin tin.

- *How many persons can be involved:* This game is best played solo or with one person guiding the activity.
- *Can it be played by a child alone:* Under adult supervision, a child can participate in placing treats and observing the dog's response.
- *What you'll need:* A muffin tin, treats, and different scents (e.g., essential oils or food extracts).

Instructions:

1. Place a treat in each cup of the muffin tin.
2. Apply different scents to some of the treats (e.g., one scent per row).
3. Show your dog the muffin tin and let them sniff and investigate.
4. Allow your dog to search for the treats and indicate the scented ones.
5. Celebrate their success when they find the scented treats by praising them and offering rewards.

Scented Ball Pit

The Scented Ball Pit game challenges your dog to find scented treats hidden in a pit filled with plastic balls.

- *How many persons can be involved:* This game is best played solo or with one person guiding the activity.
- *Can it be played by a child alone:* Under adult supervision, a child can participate in creating the ball pit and observing the dog's interaction.
- *What you'll need:* A small pool or container, plastic balls, scented treats, and a treat dispenser.

Instructions:

1. Fill the pool or container with plastic balls.
2. Hide scented treats among the balls.
3. Encourage your dog to search for and retrieve the scented treats.
4. Celebrate their success when they find a treat by praising them and offering additional treats.

Find It in the Grass

The Find It in the Grass game challenges your dog's olfactory skills as they search for treats or toys concealed in tall grass.

- *How many persons can be involved:* This game is best played solo or with one person guiding the dog.
- *Can it be played by a child alone:* Under adult supervision, a child can participate in hiding treats or toys and observing the dog's search.
- *What you'll need:* Treats or toys and an area with tall grass (such as a backyard or a designated play area).

Instructions:

1. Show your dog the treats or toys and let them sniff and see the items.
2. Hide the treats or toys in the tall grass.
3. Release your dog and give the command "Find it!"
4. Encourage your dog to search for and retrieve the hidden treats or toys.
5. Celebrate their success when they find the items by praising them and offering rewards.

Scented Blanket

The Scented Blanket game helps your dog associate a specific scent with a reward, promoting a connection between scent recognition and positive outcomes.

- *How many persons can be involved:* This game is best played solo or with one person guiding the activity.
- *Can it be played by a child alone:* Under adult supervision, a child can participate in applying scents and hiding treats.
- *What you'll need:* A blanket, treats, and a specific scent (e.g., a drop of essential oil).

Instructions:

1. Place the blanket on the ground or hold it in your hand.
2. Apply the scent to a specific area of the blanket.
3. Show your dog the blanket and let them sniff the scented area.
4. Hide treats within the folds of the blanket, including some near the scented area.
5. Encourage your dog to search for and find the treats, focusing on the scented area.
6. Celebrate their success when they locate the scented treats by praising them and offering rewards.

Scented Agility Course

The Scented Agility Course combines scent games with agility training, providing a challenging and rewarding experience for your dog's physical and mental well-being.

- *How many persons can be involved:* This game is best played solo or with one person guiding the dog through the course.
- *Can it be played by a child alone:* Under adult supervision, a child can participate in setting up the course and observing the dog's performance.
- *What you'll need:* Agility equipment (e.g., hurdles, tunnels, weave poles), scented markers (e.g., cones with different scents), and treats.

Instructions:

1. Set up an agility course using the equipment.
2. Place scented markers at different stations throughout the course.
3. Guide your dog through the course, encouraging them to follow the scent markers and complete each obstacle.
4. Reward your dog with treats and praise at the end of each successful completion.

Scented Cups

The Scented Cups game challenges your dog to identify a specific scent among various cups, enhancing their scent discrimination skills.

- *How many persons can be involved:* This game is best played solo or with one person guiding the activity.
- *Can it be played by a child alone:* Under adult supervision, a child can participate in applying scents and shuffling cups.
- *What you'll need:* Cups or containers, treats, and different scents.

Instructions:

1. Place treats under each cup and let your dog see the treats being placed.
2. Apply a different scent to the bottom of one cup.
3. Shuffle the cups around to mix up their positions.
4. Encourage your dog to indicate the cup with the specific scent by pawing or touching it.
5. Celebrate their success when they identify the correct cup by praising them and offering rewards.

Scented Sock Search

The Scented Sock Search game engages your dog's sense of smell as they search for scented socks hidden around the house.

- *How many persons can be involved:* This game is best played solo or with one person guiding the activity.
- *Can it be played by a child alone:* Under adult supervision, a child can participate in applying scents and hiding socks.
- *What you'll need:* Socks, scents (e.g., essential oils or food extracts), and treats.

Instructions:

1. Apply different scents to each sock by placing a few drops of scent on the fabric.
2. Hide the scented socks in various locations around the house.
3. Encourage your dog to search for and find the scented socks.
4. Celebrate their success when they locate a scented sock by praising them and offering treats.

Agility And Balancing Games

Agility and balancing games challenge dogs both mentally and physically. These activities involve navigating obstacles, balancing on various surfaces, and performing coordinated movements. By engaging in agility exercises, dogs improve their coordination, flexibility, and body awareness. These games also stimulate their problem-solving abilities as they figure out how to overcome obstacles. Agility and balancing activities promote overall fitness and mental acuity, keeping dogs active and engaged.

Tunnel Dash

The Tunnel Dash game involves your dog running through a tunnel, providing physical exercise and entertainment.

- *How many persons can be involved:* This game is best played solo or with one person guiding the dog.
- *Can it be played by a child alone:* No, this game is not recommended for a child to play alone. Adult supervision is necessary to guide the dog through the tunnel and ensure safety.
- *What you'll need:* A tunnel designed for dogs and treats.

Instructions:

1. Place the tunnel in an open area.
2. Encourage your dog to enter one end of the tunnel and run through to the other end.
3. Use treats to motivate your dog and guide them through the tunnel if needed.
4. Celebrate their success by praising them and offering rewards.

Jumping Hurdles

The Jumping Hurdles game challenges your dog to leap over hurdles set at different heights, promoting agility and coordination.

- *How many persons can be involved:* This game is best played solo or with one person guiding the dog.
- *Can it be played by a child alone:* No, this game is not recommended for a child to play alone. Adult supervision is necessary for adjusting the height of the hurdles and ensuring the safety of both the dog and the child.
- *What you'll need:* Adjustable hurdles or makeshift obstacles, treats, and a treat dispenser.

Instructions:

1. Set up the hurdles at a low height initially.
2. Encourage your dog to jump over the hurdles one by one.
3. Gradually increase the height of the hurdles as your dog becomes more comfortable and confident.
4. Reward your dog with treats and praise after each successful jump.

Balance Beam

The Balance Beam game challenges your dog's balance and coordination skills by walking on a narrow beam, enhancing their proprioception.

- *How many persons can be involved:* This game is best played solo or with one person guiding the dog.
- *Can it be played by a child alone:* No, this game is not recommended for a child to play alone. Adult supervision is necessary to guide the dog on the balance beam and ensure safety.
- *What you'll need:* A sturdy wooden beam or a commercial dog balance beam, treats, and a treat dispenser.

Instructions:

1. Place the balance beam on a non-slip surface.
2. Encourage your dog to walk on the beam, starting with a low height.
3. Guide them with treats and rewards for maintaining balance and walking along the beam.
4. Increase the difficulty by raising the height of the beam gradually.

Weave Poles

The Weave Poles game trains your dog to navigate through a series of closely spaced poles, promoting agility and responsiveness.

- *How many persons can be involved:* This game is best played solo or with one person guiding the dog.
- *Can it be played by a child alone:* No, this game is not recommended for a child to play alone. Adult supervision is necessary to set up the weave poles and guide the dog through the course.
- *What you'll need:* Weave poles or a set of upright poles, treats, and a treat dispenser.

Instructions:

1. Set up the weave poles in a straight line, with a slight angle if desired.
2. Lead your dog through the poles, starting with a few widely spaced poles.
3. Gradually decrease the spacing between the poles as your dog becomes more proficient.
4. Reward your dog with treats and praise after successfully weaving through the poles.

Balance Ball

The Balance Ball game challenges your dog's balance and stability by standing or walking on a large exercise ball.

- *How many persons can be involved:* This game is best played solo or with one person guiding the dog.
- *Can it be played by a child alone:* No, this game requires adult supervision and guidance due to the potential risks associated with using the balance ball.
- *What you'll need:* A large exercise ball designed for dogs, treats, and a treat dispenser.

Instructions:

1. Introduce your dog to the balance ball and allow them to investigate.
2. Encourage your dog to stand or walk on the ball, starting with a low height.
3. Use treats and rewards to reinforce their balance and stability on the ball.
4. Gradually increase the difficulty by introducing gentle movements or rolling the ball slightly.

Balancing Trick

The Balancing Trick game involves teaching your dog to balance an object on their nose or head, enhancing their focus and coordination.

- *How many persons can be involved:* This game is best played solo or with one person guiding the dog.
- *Can it be played by a child alone:* Under adult supervision, a child can participate in holding treats and observing the dog's balancing act.
- *What you'll need:* Lightweight objects that can be balanced (e.g., small plastic cones or balls), treats, and a treat dispenser.

Instructions:

1. Start by holding the object near your dog's nose and reward them for keeping their nose still.
2. Gradually place the object on their nose, rewarding them for maintaining balance.
3. Once your dog is comfortable balancing the object on their nose, introduce the cue command (e.g., "balance").
4. Reward your dog for successfully balancing the object and gradually increase the duration.

Balance Disc

The Balance Disc game helps improve your dog's balance and stability by standing or walking on a wobbly surface, enhancing core strength.

- *How many persons can be involved:* This game is best played solo or with one person guiding the dog.
- *Can it be played by a child alone:* No, this game is not recommended for a child to play alone. Adult supervision is necessary to introduce the balance disc to the dog and ensure safety.
- *What you'll need:* A balance disc designed for dogs, treats, and a treat dispenser.

Instructions:

1. Introduce your dog to the balance disc and allow them to sniff and investigate.
2. Encourage your dog to stand or walk on the balance disc.
3. Use treats to reward your dog for maintaining balance and stability on the disc.
4. Gradually increase the difficulty by introducing gentle movements or tilting the disc slightly.

Hoop Jump

The Hoop Jump game challenges your dog to jump through a hoop, enhancing their agility and coordination.

- *How many persons can be involved:* This game is best played solo or with one person guiding the dog.
- *Can it be played by a child alone:* Under adult supervision, a child can participate in holding the hoop and encouraging the dog.
- *What you'll need:* A hoop or a makeshift hoop, treats, and a treat dispenser.

Instructions:

1. Hold the hoop low to the ground and encourage your dog to walk through it.
2. Gradually raise the height of the hoop as your dog becomes comfortable.
3. Reward your dog with treats and praise after each successful jump through the hoop.
4. Increase the challenge by introducing multiple hoops or changing the angle of the hoop.

A-Frame Climb

The A-Frame Climb game challenges your dog to ascend and descend an A-frame obstacle, combining physical activity with obedience training.

- *How many persons can be involved:* This game is best played solo or with one person guiding the dog.
- *Can it be played by a child alone:* No, this game requires adult supervision and guidance due to the potential risks associated with climbing the A-frame obstacle.
- *What you'll need:* An A-frame obstacle or makeshift ramp, treats, and a treat dispenser.

Instructions:

1. Guide your dog to the base of the A-frame.
2. Encourage them to climb up the A-frame and reach the top.
3. Use treats and rewards to motivate and reinforce their climbing behavior.
4. Guide them down the other side of the A-frame and reward their successful descent.

Zigzag Cone Run

The Zigzag Cone Run game challenges your dog to navigate through a series of cones placed in a zigzag pattern, promoting agility and responsiveness.

- *How many persons can be involved:* This game is best played solo or with one person guiding the dog.
- *Can it be played by a child alone:* Under adult supervision, a child can participate in placing treats and observing the dog's navigation.
- *What you'll need:* Cones, treats, and a treat dispenser.

Instructions:

1. Set up the cones in a zigzag pattern with adequate spacing between them.
2. Lead your dog through the cones, encouraging them to weave in and out.
3. Reward your dog with treats and praise after successfully navigating the zigzag pattern.
4. Increase the difficulty by decreasing the spacing between the cones or adding more cones.

Water Games

Water games provide a refreshing and enjoyable way for dogs to cool off and have fun. Whether splashing in a pool, chasing waves at the beach, or retrieving toys from the water, these activities offer both physical and mental stimulation. Water games are particularly beneficial for dogs with joint issues or those who enjoy aquatic activities. They promote cardiovascular health, muscle strength, and mental alertness, all while keeping dogs cool and entertained.

Water Race

The Water Race game involves racing your dog in the water to see who can swim the fastest.

- *How many persons can be involved:* This game is typically played with one person racing the dog in the water.
- *Can it be played by a child alone:* No, this game involves water and swimming, making it more suitable for adult supervision to ensure safety.
- *What you'll need:* Open water area or a swimming pool.

Instructions:

1. Stand at one end of the water area or pool, and encourage your dog to stand at the other end.
2. Give a signal or command to start, and both you and your dog swim towards each other.
3. Celebrate and reward your dog for reaching you, and repeat the race multiple times.

Water Fetch

The Water Fetch game is a classic game of fetch in the water.

- *How many persons can be involved:* This game is typically played solo or with one person throwing the toy into the water.
- *Can it be played by a child alone:* No, this game involves water and is not recommended to be played by a child alone. Adult supervision is essential for the safety of both the child and the dog.
- *What you'll need:* Floating toys (e.g., rubber toys, balls, or floating sticks).

Instructions:

1. Stand in shallow water and throw the toy into the water.
2. Encourage your dog to swim out and retrieve the toy.
3. When your dog brings the toy back, reward them and throw the toy again.

Sprinkler Limbo

The Sprinkler Limbo game combines the fun of a sprinkler with a limbo challenge for your dog to duck under the water.

- *How many persons can be involved:* This game can be played solo, with one person controlling the sprinkler.
- *Can it be played by a child alone:* Yes, a child can play this game alone with adult supervision to ensure the proper use of the sprinkler.
- *What you'll need:* Garden hose with a spray nozzle or a low sprinkler.

Instructions:

1. Set up the hose or sprinkler to create a low, arched stream of water.
2. Encourage your dog to walk or run under the water stream without touching it.
3. Reward your dog for successfully limbo-ing under the water and repeat the game.

Water Obstacle Course

The Water Obstacle Course game involves creating a course with various water-based obstacles for your dog to navigate through.

- *How many persons can be involved:* This game is typically played with one person guiding the dog through the water course.
- *Can it be played by a child alone:* No, this game involves water and guiding the dog through obstacles, making it more suitable for adult supervision to ensure safety.
- *What you'll need:* Floating objects, pool noodles, hoops, and other water-safe materials.

Instructions:

1. Set up a course in the water with floating objects, pool noodles, and hoops.
2. Guide your dog through the course, encouraging them to jump over, swim under, or weave through the obstacles.
3. Reward your dog for completing each section of the course and celebrate their success.

Hose Sprinkler Fun

The Hose Sprinkler Fun game involves playing with a hose or sprinkler for your dog to chase and run through the water.

- *How many persons can be involved:* This game can be played with one person controlling the hose or sprinkler.
- *Can it be played by a child alone:* Yes, a child can play this game alone with adult supervision to ensure the proper use of the hose or sprinkler.
- *What you'll need:* Garden hose with a spray nozzle or a sprinkler.

Instructions:

1. Set up the hose or sprinkler in an open area.
2. Turn on the water to create a gentle spray or sprinkle.
3. Encourage your dog to chase and run through the water.
4. Join in the fun by running alongside your dog or spraying water towards them.

Water Slide

The Water Slide game involves creating a gentle water slide for your dog to slide into the water.

- *How many persons can be involved:* This game is typically played solo, with one person encouraging the dog to use the water slide.
- *Can it be played by a child alone:* No, this game involves water and potentially elevated structures, making it more suitable for adult supervision to ensure safety.
- *What you'll need:* A pool slide or a makeshift slide with a water source.

Instructions:

1. Set up the pool slide or create a makeshift slide with a water source.
2. Encourage your dog to climb the slide and slide down into the water.
3. Reward your dog for their brave slide and repeat the game.

Splash and Retrieve

The Splash and Retrieve game involves throwing a floating toy into the water for your dog to retrieve.

- *How many persons can be involved:* This game is typically played solo or with one person throwing the toy into the water.
- *Can it be played by a child alone:* No, this game involves water and is not recommended to be played by a child alone. Adult supervision is essential for the safety of both the child and the dog.
- *What you'll need:* Floating toys (e.g., rubber toys, balls, or frisbees).

Instructions:

1. Stand near the water's edge and throw the floating toy into the water.
2. Encourage your dog to swim out and retrieve the toy.
3. Once your dog brings the toy back, reward them with praise and play again.

Water Tug-of-War

The Water Tug-of-War game is a water-based version of the classic game, using a water-soaked rope or floating tug toy.

- *How many persons can be involved:* This game is typically played with one person holding the rope or toy.
- *Can it be played by a child alone:* No, this game involves water and tug-of-war, making it more suitable for adult supervision to ensure safety.
- *What you'll need:* Water-soaked rope or floating tug toy.

Instructions:

1. Stand in shallow water and hold one end of the rope or toy.
2. Encourage your dog to grab onto the other end and engage in a friendly tug-of-war.
3. Be mindful of your dog's strength and size to ensure a safe and enjoyable game.

Water Maze

The Water Maze game challenges your dog to navigate through a series of floating obstacles in the water.

- *How many persons can be involved:* This game is typically played solo or with one person guiding the dog through the water maze.
- *Can it be played by a child alone:* No, this game involves water and guiding the dog through a maze, making it more suitable for adult supervision to ensure safety.
- *What you'll need:* Floating objects (e.g., pool noodles, floating toys, or buoys).

Instructions:

1. Place the floating objects in the water, creating a maze-like structure.
2. Guide your dog through the maze, encouraging them to swim around or through the obstacles.
3. Reward your dog with praise and treats for successfully navigating the water maze.

Water Polo

The Water Polo game is a canine version of the popular sport, involving passing and scoring goals with a floating ball.

- *How many persons can be involved:* This game is typically played with at least two persons, one on each team.
- *Can it be played by a child alone:* No, this game involves water and coordination between players, making it more suitable for adult involvement.
- *What you'll need:* A floating ball and two goals (could be floating objects or markers).

Instructions:

1. Place the goals at opposite ends of the water area.
2. Pass the floating ball between you and your dog, attempting to score goals by getting the ball into the opposing goal.
3. Celebrate each goal and encourage fair play by taking turns between you and your dog.

Focus Games

Focus games are designed to improve a dog's ability to concentrate, follow cues, and maintain attention. These activities challenge their cognitive skills and promote mental agility. By practicing focus games, dogs learn to ignore distractions and focus on the task at hand. This enhances their obedience, responsiveness, and overall trainability. Focus games also provide mental stimulation, preventing boredom and fostering a deeper bond between dogs and their owners.

Find It

The Find It game encourages your dog to use their nose to locate hidden treats or toys.

- *How many persons can be involved:* This game can be played with one person hiding treats or toys for the dog to find.
- *Can it be played by a child alone:* Yes, this game can be played by a child alone as it involves hiding treats and commanding the dog.
- *What you'll need:* Treats or toys and a designated hiding spot.

Instructions:

1. Show your dog a treat or toy and let them sniff it.
2. While your dog is watching, hide the treat or toy in a nearby location.
3. Say "Find it!" or a similar command and encourage your dog to search for the hidden item.
4. Reward your dog when they find the item and repeat the game with different hiding spots.

Hide and Seek

Hide and Seek game encourages your dog to find you or another person in a designated area.

- *How many persons can be involved:* This game typically involves one person hiding and another person calling the dog.
- *Can it be played by a child alone:* Yes, a child can play this game alone, hiding and calling the dog.
- *What you'll need:* Treats and a hiding spot.

Instructions:

1. Ask your dog to stay or have someone hold them.
2. Find a hiding spot in the designated area and call your dog's name or use a command.
3. When your dog finds you, reward them with treats and praise.
4. Repeat the game with different hiding spots and participants.

Cup Game

The Cup Game challenges your dog to find the treat under one of several cups.

- *How many persons can be involved:* This game can be played with one person hiding treats under cups and rewarding the dog.
- *Can it be played by a child alone:* Yes, this game can be played by a child alone as it involves simple actions and treats.
- *What you'll need:* Cups (3-5) and treats.

Instructions:

1. Show your dog a treat and let them see you place it under one of the cups.
2. Shuffle the cups around to mix up their positions.
3. Encourage your dog to find the cup with the treat by sniffing or pawing at it.
4. Reward your dog when they choose the correct cup and repeat the game with different arrangements.

Follow the Finger

The Follow the Finger game teaches your dog to track your finger with their eyes and maintain focus.

- *How many persons can be involved:* This game can be played with one person moving their finger and rewarding the dog.
- *Can it be played by a child alone:* Yes, this game can be played by a child alone as it involves simple movements and treats.
- *What you'll need:* Treats and a quiet environment.

Instructions:

1. Hold a treat in one hand and extend your other hand with your finger pointing.
2. Slowly move your finger in different directions while keeping your dog's attention.
3. Reward your dog with the treat when they follow your finger with their eyes.
4. Gradually increase the difficulty by moving your finger faster or in more complex patterns.

Name Recognition

The Name Recognition game involves teaching your dog to respond to their name.

- *How many persons can be involved:* This game can be played with one person calling the dog by its name.
- *Can it be played by a child alone:* Yes, this game can be played by a child alone as it only requires calling the dog's name and giving treats.
- *What you'll need:* Treats and a quiet environment.

Instructions:

1. Say your dog's name in a calm and clear tone.
2. As soon as they look at you or respond, reward them with a treat and praise.
3. Repeat this exercise in different locations and gradually increase distractions.

Guess the Hand

Guess the Hand game challenges your dog to choose the correct hand holding a treat.

- *How many persons can be involved:* This game involves one person holding the treats.
- *Can it be played by a child alone:* Yes, a child can play this game alone, holding the treats and guiding the dog's choice.
- *What you'll need:* Treats and two closed hands.

Instructions:

1. Show your dog a treat and place it in one of your hands.
2. Close both hands, making sure your dog can't see the treat.
3. Extend your hands toward your dog and encourage them to choose the hand with the treat.
4. Reward your dog when they choose the correct hand and repeat the game multiple times.

Stairway Game

The Stairway Game helps your dog focus on climbing or descending stairs in a controlled manner.

- *How many persons can be involved:* This game can be played with one person leading the dog up or down the stairs.
- *Can it be played by a child alone:* No, this game may be more suitable for adult supervision, especially if the dog is large or the stairs are steep.
- *What you'll need:* A staircase and treats.

Instructions:

1. Stand at the top or bottom of the staircase with your dog on a leash.
2. Begin to climb or descend the stairs slowly, encouraging your dog to follow you.
3. Reward your dog with a treat and praise for each step they take correctly.
4. Repeat the exercise, gradually increasing the speed and adding more steps.

The Statue Game

The Statue Game improves your dog's impulse control by teaching them to remain still.

- *How many persons can be involved:* This game is typically played with one person instructing the dog.
- *Can it be played by a child alone:* Yes, a child can play this game alone, instructing the dog to stay still and rewarding them accordingly.
- *What you'll need:* Treats and a quiet environment.

Instructions:

1. Ask your dog to sit or stand in front of you.
2. Say "Statue" or a similar command and hold your hand up like a stop sign.
3. Count to a few seconds and reward your dog with a treat for staying still.
4. Gradually increase the duration before rewarding and introduce distractions.

Memory Game

Memory Game challenges your dog to remember the location of hidden treats or toys.

- *How many persons can be involved:* This game typically involves one person hiding the treats or toys.
- *Can it be played by a child alone:* Yes, a child can play this game alone, hiding the treats or toys and guiding the dog.
- *What you'll need:* Treats or toys and several cups or objects to cover them.

Instructions:

1. Show your dog a treat or toy and let them sniff it.
2. While your dog is watching, place the treat or toy under one of the cups or objects.
3. Shuffle the cups or objects around to mix up their positions.
4. Encourage your dog to find the hidden treat or toy by uncovering the correct cup or object.
5. Reward your dog when they uncover the correct one and repeat the game with different arrangements.

Time Out

Time Out game teaches your dog self-control by rewarding them for staying calm during distractions.

- *How many persons can be involved:* This game typically involves one person managing the dog and introducing distractions.
- *Can it be played by a child alone:* Yes, a child can play this game alone, managing the dog and rewarding them for calm behavior.
- *What you'll need:* Treats and distractions (e.g., toys, other people).

Instructions:

1. Begin with your dog on a leash and introduce a distraction, such as someone walking by or a toy being tossed.
2. When your dog remains calm and doesn't react to the distraction, reward them with a treat and praise.
3. Gradually increase the level of distractions and reward your dog for maintaining composure.

Impulse Control Games

Impulse control games help dogs develop self-discipline and restraint in various situations. These activities require them to resist immediate impulses, wait for cues, and make thoughtful decisions. By practicing impulse control, dogs learn to control their impulses, reduce unwanted behaviors, and improve their ability to handle exciting or challenging situations. These games also promote patience, self-control, and a greater sense of calmness in dogs, contributing to their overall well-being and behavior.

Red Light, Green Light

This fun game helps your dog enhance self-control, halting when you say "Red Light" and moving on "Green Light."

- *How many persons can be involved:* Typically, this game involves one person managing the leash and giving commands.
- *Can it be played by a child alone:* Absolutely, a child can play this game solo, practicing impulse control cues with the dog.
- *What you'll need:* Treats and a clear space to move around.

Instructions:

1. Walk with your dog on a leash and intermittently stop.
2. Say "Red Light" and stop walking, waiting for your dog to also stop.
3. Reward your dog with a treat and say "Green Light" to resume walking.
4. Repeat the game, gradually extending the duration of stops.

Toy Tug with Control

This game helps your dog develop impulse control during a game of tug-of-war.

- *How many persons can be involved:* Typically, this game involves one person playing tug-of-war with the dog.
- *Can it be played by a child alone:* Yes, a child can play this game alone, engaging in tug-of-war and practicing impulse control cues.
- *What you'll need:* A sturdy tug toy.

Instructions:

1. Initiate a game of tug-of-war with your dog using the tug toy.
2. Pause the game periodically and ask your dog to "Drop it" or "Leave it."
3. Reward your dog with praise and a treat when they release the toy.
4. Resume the game and repeat the process to reinforce impulse control.

Leave it and Take it

This game teaches your dog to leave an item on the ground until you give them permission to take it.

- *How many persons can be involved:* Typically, this game involves one person presenting items to the dog.
- *Can it be played by a child alone:* Yes, a child can play this game alone, presenting items and practicing "Leave it" cues.
- *What you'll need:* Treats and objects your dog finds tempting (e.g., toys, food).

Instructions:

1. Show your dog a tempting item in your hand.
2. Say "Leave it" in a firm but calm voice and close your hand.
3. Wait for your dog to stop showing interest in the item.
4. Open your hand and reward your dog with a treat.
5. Practice this game with different objects and gradually increase the difficulty.

Wait for the Food

This game teaches your dog to wait patiently for their food until you give them the cue to eat.

- *How many persons can be involved:* Typically, this game involves one person managing the food bowl and cueing the dog.
- *Can it be played by a child alone:* Yes, a child can play this game alone, managing the food bowl and giving cues to the dog.
- *What you'll need:* Your dog's food bowl and treats.

Instructions:

1. Hold your dog's food bowl and ask them to sit or wait.
2. Gradually lower the food bowl while keeping it out of your dog's reach.
3. If your dog remains calm and waits, give them a release cue (e.g., "Okay") to start eating.
4. Reward your dog with treats and praise for waiting calmly.

Impulse Control with Food

This game teaches your dog to resist the allure of food until given permission to eat.

- *How many persons can be involved:* Typically, this game involves one person managing the food bowl and treats.
- *Can it be played by a child alone:* Certainly, a child can play this game solo, handling the food bowl and practicing impulse control cues with the dog.
- *What you'll need:* Treats and your dog's food bowl.

Instructions:

1. Place your dog's food bowl on the ground.
2. Hold a treat in your hand and cover the food bowl with your other hand.
3. State "Wait" or a similar command and wait for your dog to remain calm.
4. Release your dog with a cue (e.g., "Okay") to eat their food and reward them with a treat.

Drop It

This instructive game teaches your dog to release an item on command.

- *How many persons can be involved:* Primarily, this game involves one person interacting with the dog and managing treats.
- *Can it be played by a child alone:* Absolutely, a child can play this game solo, engaging in play with the dog and practicing the "Drop it" cue.
- *What you'll need:* Treats and an item your dog enjoys playing with (e.g., a ball, toy).

Instructions:

1. Initiate play with your dog using the item they enjoy.
2. Say "Drop it" and reveal a treat in your hand.
3. When your dog lets go of the item, reward them with the treat and praise.
4. Repeat the game, gradually increasing the duration of holding the item before issuing the command.

Impulse Control with Doorways

This game helps your dog learn to wait at doorways until given permission to pass through.

- *How many persons can be involved:* Typically, this game involves one person managing the leash and door.
- *Can it be played by a child alone:* Yes, a child can play this game alone, managing the leash and practicing door etiquette with the dog.
- *What you'll need:* Treats and a doorway.

Instructions:

1. Stand in front of a doorway with your dog on a leash.
2. Say "Wait" or a similar command and slowly open the door.
3. If your dog tries to pass through, gently close the door and say "Oops."
4. When your dog remains calm and waits, give them a release cue (e.g., "Okay") to pass through.
5. Reward your dog with treats and praise for waiting patiently.

Name Game

This game helps your dog practice impulse control by waiting until you call their name before giving attention or treats.

- *How many persons can be involved:* Typically, this game involves one person interacting with the dog.
- *Can it be played by a child alone:* Yes, a child can play this game alone, calling the dog by name and rewarding attention.
- *What you'll need:* Treats.

Instructions:

1. Sit or kneel in front of your dog with treats in your hand.
2. Say your dog's name and wait for them to make eye contact or focus on you.
3. Once your dog is attentive, reward them with a treat and praise.
4. Repeat this game, gradually increasing the duration of eye contact before giving the reward.

It's Your Choice

This engaging game encourages your dog to make positive decisions by resisting distractions and focusing on you.

- *How many persons can be involved:* Ideally, this game involves one person presenting distractions and managing the treats.
- *Can it be played by a child alone:* Yes, a child can play this game solo, introducing distractions and practicing impulse control cues with the dog.
- *What you'll need:* Treats and distractions (e.g., toys, food).

Instructions:

1. Hold a treat in your hand and present it to your dog.
2. If your dog attempts to grab the treat without permission, close your hand.
3. Wait for your dog to back away or lose interest in the treat.
4. Open your hand and reward your dog when they exhibit self-control.
5. Repeat the game, gradually increasing the complexity of distractions.

Boundary Game

This educational game teaches your dog to stay within a designated area until given permission to leave.

- *How many persons can be involved:* Primarily, this game involves one person managing the boundary and giving commands.
- *Can it be played by a child alone:* Certainly, a child can play this game solo, setting up the boundary and practicing impulse control cues with the dog.
- *What you'll need:* Treats and a designated boundary (e.g., a mat or boundary markers).

Instructions:

1. Position your dog's bed or a mat on the floor as the designated boundary.
2. Ask your dog to go to the boundary and issue the command "Stay" or "Boundary."
3. Reward your dog with treats and praise for remaining within the boundary.
4. Gradually increase the duration before issuing the release cue.

Mental Health And Cognitive Games

Mental health and cognitive games are essential for keeping a dog's mind sharp and engaged. These activities stimulate their problem-solving skills, memory, and cognitive functions. By engaging in mental exercises, dogs stay mentally alert, prevent cognitive decline, and maintain overall mental well-being. Mental health games also provide a sense of accomplishment and fulfillment for dogs as they successfully solve puzzles or complete tasks. These games are particularly beneficial for senior dogs or those with limited physical activity, offering a fun and rewarding way to keep their minds active.

Shell Game

The Shell Game tests your dog's memory and scent-tracking abilities as they aim to locate the hidden treat under one of three cups.

- *How many persons can be involved:* Mainly involves one person managing the cups and treats.
- *Can it be played by a child alone:* Possible for a child to play solo, shuffling the cups and practicing memory and scent-tracking cues with the dog.
- *What you'll need:* Three identical cups or bowls and a treat.

Instructions:

1. Show your dog the treat and then place it under one of the cups.
2. Shuffle the cups around to confuse your dog.
3. Encourage your dog to use their nose or paw to indicate which cup they believe the treat is hidden under.
4. Reward your dog when they choose the correct cup by praising them and offering the treat as a reward.

Toy Puzzle Box

A toy puzzle box challenges your dog's problem-solving skills by requiring them to figure out how to open compartments or drawers to access hidden treats or toys.

- *How many persons can be involved:* Primarily involves one person guiding the dog.
- *Can it be played by a child alone:* Possible for a child to play solo, setting up the puzzle box and encouraging the dog to solve it.
- *What you'll need:* A toy puzzle box or a container with compartments, treats or toys.

Instructions:

1. Introduce your dog to the toy puzzle box and let them explore it.
2. Place treats or toys in the compartments or drawers of the puzzle box.
3. Encourage your dog to interact with the puzzle box and figure out how to open each compartment to retrieve the rewards.
4. Provide guidance or hints if necessary to help your dog solve the puzzle.
5. Celebrate when your dog successfully opens the compartments and gets the treats or toys.

Doggie Soccer

Doggie Soccer combines physical exercise and mental stimulation as your dog learns to push a ball towards a goal.

- *How many persons can be involved:* Primarily involves one person guiding the dog.
- *Can it be played by a child alone:* Possible for a child to play solo, guiding the dog to interact with the ball and goal.
- *What you'll need:* A large, soft ball and a goal (can be makeshift or purchased).

Instructions:

1. Introduce the ball to your dog and let them interact with it.
2. Encourage your dog to use their nose or paws to push the ball towards the goal.
3. Guide your dog's actions and reward them when they successfully make contact with the ball.
4. Gradually increase the distance between your dog and the goal to make it more challenging.
5. Celebrate and reward your dog when they score a goal.

Mimic Me

This game tests your dog's ability to imitate your actions.

- *How many persons can be involved:* Primarily involves one person demonstrating actions and rewarding the dog.
- *Can it be played by a child alone:* Absolutely, a child can play solo, demonstrating actions and rewarding the dog's mimicry.
- *What you'll need:* Treats and a space for movement.

Instructions:

1. Perform a simple action, such as clapping your hands or tapping your foot.
2. Give your dog a cue, such as "Do it" or "Copy me."
3. Encourage your dog to imitate your action by performing a similar behavior.
4. Reward your dog when they successfully mimic your action.
5. Repeat with different actions and gradually increase the complexity.

Tunnel Crawl

Tunnel Crawl game challenges your dog to crawl through a narrow tunnel.

- *How many persons can be involved:* Mainly involves one person guiding the dog.
- *Can it be played by a child alone:* Possible for a child to play solo, guiding the dog through the tunnel.
- *What you'll need:* A low and narrow tunnel designed for dogs, treats, and a treat dispenser.

Instructions:

1. Guide your dog to the entrance of the tunnel and encourage them to crawl through.
2. Use treats and rewards to motivate and guide them through the tunnel.
3. Celebrate their success at the other end of the tunnel by praising them and offering treats.
4. Gradually increase the length or add curves to the tunnel for added challenge.

The "Clean Up" Game

The "Clean Up" game teaches your dog to tidy up their toys and promotes obedience and cooperation.

- *How many persons can be involved:* Primarily involves one person guiding the dog.
- *Can it be played by a child alone:* Possible for a child to play solo, teaching the dog the "Clean up" command and rewarding the behavior.
- *What you'll need:* Your dog's toys and a designated container for toy storage.

Instructions:

1. Teach your dog the command "Clean up" or any similar cue associated with the task.
2. Encourage your dog to pick up a toy and bring it to the designated container.
3. Reward and praise your dog each time they successfully place a toy in the container.
4. Gradually increase the difficulty by adding more toys and reinforcing the command.
5. Celebrate and reward your dog when they tidy up their toys.

Shape Sorter

This game challenges your dog's problem-solving abilities by sorting objects based on shape.

- *How many persons can be involved:* Primarily involves one person demonstrating and guiding the dog.
- *Can it be played by a child alone:* Possible for a child to play solo, demonstrating how to place objects and encouraging the dog to solve the puzzle.
- *What you'll need:* A shape sorter toy or several objects of different shapes.

Instructions:

1. Introduce your dog to the shape sorter toy or the objects with different shapes.
2. Show your dog how to place the objects into the corresponding holes or containers based on shape.
3. Encourage your dog to explore and figure out how to fit the objects into the right places.
4. Celebrate and reward your dog when they successfully complete the task.

Which Hand

This game challenges your dog's ability to use their sense of smell to identify which hand contains the hidden treat.

- *How many persons can be involved:* Primarily involves one person managing the treats and hands.
- *Can it be played by a child alone:* Absolutely, a child can play this game solo, hiding treats and practicing scent-tracking cues with the dog.
- *What you'll need:* Treats and your hands.

Instructions:

1. Show your dog the treat and let them sniff it.
2. Close your hands, one with the treat and one empty.
3. Offer both closed hands to your dog, palms facing up.
4. Encourage your dog to choose the correct hand by sniffing and pawing at it.
5. Celebrate and reward your dog when they choose the correct hand.

Target Stick

Target Stick game involves teaching your dog to touch a target stick with their nose or paw.

- *How many persons can be involved:* Mainly involves one person guiding the dog.
- *Can it be played by a child alone:* Possible for a child to play solo, using the target stick to guide the dog.
- *What you'll need:* A target stick (e.g., a stick with a ball or a clicker), treats, and a treat dispenser.

Instructions:

1. Present the target stick to your dog and reward them for touching it with their nose or paw.
2. Gradually move the target stick to different positions and reward your dog for targeting it.
3. Introduce the cue command (e.g., "touch") and reward your dog for targeting on command.
4. Increase the difficulty by placing the target stick in higher or more challenging positions.

Staircase Challenge

This game challenges your dog's cognitive skills by teaching them to navigate stairs using commands.

- *How many persons can be involved:* Mainly involves one person giving commands and managing treats.
- *Can it be played by a child alone:* Possible for a child to play solo, guiding the dog up the stairs and practicing obedience commands.
- *What you'll need:* A staircase.

Instructions:

1. Start with a few steps on the staircase and ask your dog to wait at the bottom.
2. Climb up the stairs and call your dog to "Come" or use a specific command.
3. Encourage your dog to climb the stairs and reward them with treats and praise.
4. Gradually increase the number of stairs your dog needs to climb.

Indoor And Outdoor Games

Whether indoors or outdoors, there are countless games to keep dogs entertained and active. Indoor games such as hide-and-seek, gentle tug-of-war, or interactive toys provide mental stimulation and encourage physical activity. Outdoor activities like fetch, exploring new trails, or running through agility courses offer opportunities for dogs to release energy and enjoy the great outdoors. Both indoor and outdoor games cater to a dog's natural instincts, providing a well-rounded playtime experience that promotes physical fitness and mental well-being.

Simon Says

Simon Says is a game that tests your dog's obedience and listening skills.

- *How many persons can be involved:* This game is typically played with one person giving commands and rewarding the dog.
- *Can it be played by a child alone:* Yes, a child can give commands and reward the dog.
- *What you'll need:* Treats.

Instructions:

1. Give your dog a command, such as "Sit" or "Lie Down."
2. If your dog performs the command correctly, reward them with a treat.
3. If you say "Simon Says" before the command, your dog should obey and receive a treat.
4. If you give a command without saying "Simon Says" and your dog performs it, they should not receive a treat.

Sock Tug

Sock Tug is a gentle game that allows your dog to engage in interactive play with a sock.

- *How many persons can be involved:* This game is typically played with one person holding the sock and one dog tugging on the other end.
- *Can it be played by a child alone:* Yes, a child can engage in this game with the dog.
- *What you'll need:* A clean sock.

Instructions:

1. Hold one end of the sock while your dog grabs the other end with their mouth.
2. Gently tug back and forth, allowing your dog to pull on the sock.
3. Maintain a relaxed grip and avoid excessive pulling to prevent the sock from tearing.
4. Reward your dog with praise and playtime for participating.

Obstacle Course

Creating an obstacle course in your house provides physical exercise and mental stimulation for your dog.

- *How many persons can be involved:* This game is typically played with one person guiding the dog through the course.
- *Can it be played by a child alone:* Yes, a child can set up the obstacles and guide the dog through the course.
- *What you'll need:* Household items like pillows, chairs, and tunnels.

Instructions:

1. Arrange pillows to create hurdles for your dog to jump over.
2. Place chairs or tables in a zigzag pattern to create weaving poles.
3. Use blankets or tunnels for your dog to crawl through.
4. Guide your dog through the obstacle course, using treats and praise as motivation.

Balloon Volleyball

Balloon Volleyball is a game that promotes physical activity and coordination as your dog tries to keep a balloon from touching the ground.

- *How many persons can be involved:* This game is typically played with one person tossing the balloon and interacting with the dog.
- *Can it be played by a child alone:* Yes, a child can toss the balloon and engage the dog in the play.
- *What you'll need:* A balloon and an open space in your house.

Instructions:

1. Blow up a balloon and lightly toss it in the air.
2. Encourage your dog to use their paws or nose to keep the balloon from touching the ground.
3. Engage in a playful back-and-forth volley with your dog.
4. Celebrate and reward your dog when they successfully keep the balloon in the air.

Bottle Bowling

Bottle Bowling is a game that allows your dog to use their nose or paws to knock down plastic bottles.

- *How many persons can be involved:* This game can be played solo or with one person setting up the bottles and encouraging the dog.
- *Can it be played by a child alone:* Yes, a child can set up the bottles and encourage the dog to play.
- *What you'll need:* Empty plastic bottles and treats.

Instructions:

1. Set up empty plastic bottles in a triangular formation, similar to a bowling alley.
2. Place treats or kibble inside some of the bottles.
3. Encourage your dog to knock down the bottles to find the hidden treats.
4. Reward your dog with treats for successful knockdowns.

Doggie Basketball

Doggie Basketball is a game that combines physical activity with mental stimulation as your dog learns to put a ball into a basket.

- *How many persons can be involved:* This game can be played solo or with one person guiding the dog.
- *Can it be played by a child alone:* Yes, a child can set up the basket, encourage the dog, and reward them.
- *What you'll need:* A small ball and a basket or hoop.

Instructions:

1. Place the basket or hoop at a suitable height for your dog.
2. Show your dog the ball and encourage them to grab it with their mouth.
3. Guide your dog to bring the ball to the basket and drop it inside.
4. Reward your dog with treats and praise when they successfully make a basket.

Treat Limbo

Treat Limbo is a game that tests your dog's flexibility and coordination as they navigate under a "limbo stick" to retrieve treats.

- *How many persons can be involved:* This game is typically played with one person holding the limbo stick and encouraging the dog.
- *Can it be played by a child alone:* Yes, a child can set up the limbo stick, encourage the dog, and reward them.
- *What you'll need:* A broomstick or a similar object and treats.

Instructions:

1. Hold the broomstick horizontally at a low height, allowing your dog to easily go under it.
2. Encourage your dog to go under the stick by luring them with a treat.
3. Gradually lower the stick to make it more challenging for your dog to pass under.
4. Reward your dog with treats when they successfully navigate under the stick.
5. Adjust the height of the stick based on your dog's abilities.

Musical Mats

Musical Mats is a dog-friendly version of musical chairs that tests your dog's listening and obedience skills.

- *How many persons can be involved:* This game is typically played with one person guiding the dog and controlling the music.
- *Can it be played by a child alone:* Yes, a child can guide the dog and control the music.
- *What you'll need:* Mats or towels and treats.

Instructions:

1. Place mats or towels in a circle on the floor, one fewer than the number of participants.
2. Play music and have your dog walk or run around the circle of mats.
3. When the music stops, call out a command like "Sit" or "Down."
4. Your dog should quickly obey the command and sit on a mat.
5. Remove one mat each round until only one mat is left, and the last dog sitting on the mat wins a treat.

Newspaper Search

The Newspaper Search game engages your dog's sense of smell as they search for hidden treats among crumpled newspapers.

- How many persons can be involved: This game is typically played with one person hiding treats and encouraging the dog.
- Can it be played by a child alone: Yes, a child can crumple newspapers, hide treats, and engage the dog in the search.
- What you'll need: Newspapers and treats.

Instructions:

1. Crumple several sheets of newspaper into balls.
2. Hide treats within the crumpled newspapers.
3. Scatter the newspaper balls around the room.
4. Encourage your dog to sniff out and find the treats hidden within the newspapers.

Treat Maze

The Treat Maze game challenges your dog's problem-solving abilities as they navigate through a maze to find hidden treats.

- *How many persons can be involved:* This game is typically played with one person setting up the maze and guiding the dog.
- *Can it be played by a child alone:* Yes, a child can create the maze, place treats, and guide the dog.
- *What you'll need:* Cardboard, scissors, treats, and tape.

Instructions:

1. Cut a piece of cardboard into a maze-like structure with dead ends and multiple pathways.
2. Place treats at different points within the maze.
3. Show your dog a treat and let them see you place it at the start of the maze.
4. Encourage your dog to navigate through the maze to find the treats.
5. Guide them with verbal cues or gestures if needed and reward them when they locate the treats.

Teaching To Play With Kids

Introducing dogs to play with children is a wonderful way to foster positive interactions and strengthen the bond between them. These activities teach children to interact gently and respectfully with dogs, promoting empathy and understanding. Dogs benefit from socialization with children, learning to be patient, tolerant, and gentle. Playing with kids also enhances a dog's social skills and confidence, as they navigate new experiences and build trust with young companions. These interactions create lasting memories and joyful moments for both dogs and children, fostering a loving and harmonious relationship.

Bubble Fun

Playing with bubbles is an entertaining activity that can capture your dog's attention and engage your child in interactive play.

- *How many persons can be involved:* This activity can involve a child blowing bubbles while interacting with a dog.
- *Can it be played by a child alone:* Yes, a child can blow bubbles while the dog interacts with them but supervision is recommended to ensure the safety of both the child and the dog.
- *What you'll need:* Bubble solution and bubble wand.

Instructions:

1. Create a safe and open space for bubble play.
2. Have your child blow bubbles using the bubble wand.
3. Encourage your dog to chase and pop the bubbles.
4. Celebrate and reward your dog's interaction with the bubbles.
5. Ensure that the bubble solution is non-toxic and safe for your dog to avoid ingestion.

Puppet Show

Puppet Show is an imaginative game where your child can create a puppet show and involve your dog as an audience member.

- *How many persons can be involved:* This activity involves a child performing a puppet show with a dog as the audience.
- *Can it be played by a child alone:* Yes, a child can create and perform the puppet show while the dog watches.
- *What you'll need:* Puppets or stuffed animals.

Instructions:

1. Have your child set up a small puppet show area using a table or cardboard box.
2. Encourage your child to put on a puppet show, telling a story or acting out a scene.
3. Invite your dog to sit or lie down as the audience member, watching the show.
4. Praise your dog for their calm behavior and engage them with treats or gentle petting during breaks.
5. Enjoy the creative performance together.

Ball Pit Fun

Ball pits are a playful and interactive way for your child and your dog to enjoy sensory stimulation and gentle physical activity.

- *How many persons can be involved:* This activity can involve a child and a dog, with supervision.
- *Can it be played by a child alone:* No, this activity requires supervision to ensure the safety of both the child and the dog.
- *What you'll need:* A small inflatable pool or a large container filled with soft, child-safe balls.

Instructions:

1. Create a safe and contained area using the inflatable pool or a designated space.
2. Fill the pool or container with soft balls.
3. Encourage your child and your dog to explore and play within the ball pit.
4. Use toys or treats to engage your dog, encouraging them to interact with the balls.
5. Supervise the playtime to ensure safety and prevent swallowing of the balls.

Paw Painting

Paw Painting is a creative activity where your child and dog can collaborate to create unique artwork using their paws.

- *How many persons can be involved:* This activity involves a child guiding the dog to create paw prints.
- *Can it be played by a child alone:* Yes, a child can guide the dog to create paw prints while supervising the activity.
- *What you'll need:* Non-toxic and washable paint, large paper or canvas, water, and towels.

Instructions:

1. Prepare the painting area by laying down the large paper or canvas.
2. Dip your dog's paw in a small amount of non-toxic paint.
3. Guide your dog's paw onto the paper or canvas to create paw prints.
4. Have your child use their hands or brushes to add additional artistic elements.
5. Repeat the process with different colors and patterns, creating a collaborative masterpiece.

Musical Sit

Musical Sit is a variation of the classic musical chairs game that involves your dog and your kid.

- *How many persons can be involved:* This activity involves three participants: a child, a dog, and another participant to lead the game.
- *Can it be played by a child alone:* No, another participant is needed to lead the game and interact with the dog.
- *What you'll need:* Chairs or mats, and some upbeat music.

Instructions:

1. Arrange chairs or mats in a circle, facing outward.
2. Start playing upbeat music and have your child walk or dance around the chairs.
3. When the music stops, your child must find a chair and sit down, and your dog must also sit beside them.
4. Remove one chair each round, and continue playing until there's only one chair left.
5. The last round can be a race between your child and your dog to see who can sit down first.

Freeze Dance with Furry Friends

Freeze Dance with Furry Friends adds a playful twist to the classic game of Freeze Dance, incorporating your dog into the fun.

- *How many persons can be involved:* This activity involves three participants: a child, a dog, and another participant to lead the game.
- *Can it be played by a child alone:* No, another participant is needed to lead the game and interact with the dog.
- *What you'll need:* Upbeat music, a clear space for dancing.

Instructions:

1. Play lively music and encourage your child to dance around with the dog.
2. At random intervals, pause the music and shout "Freeze!"
3. Both the child and the dog must freeze in place until the music resumes.
4. The other participant (such as a parent or sibling) can lead the game, call out "Freeze," and interact with the dog.
5. Reward the dog with treats or praise for participating and freezing on cue.
6. Continue the game, varying the dance moves and freeze moments.
7. Have fun watching your child and dog boogie down together in this interactive dance game.
8. Ensure that the dancing space is safe and free of obstacles.

Agility Tunnel Races

Set up an agility tunnel and have your child and dog race through it, promoting agility and speed.

- *How many persons can be involved:* This activity involves a child and a dog.
- *Can it be played by a child alone:* Yes, a child can set up the agility tunnel and race through it with the dog.
- *What you'll need:* An agility tunnel.

Instructions:

1. Set up the agility tunnel in a clear space inside your home.
2. Have your child and dog stand on opposite ends of the tunnel.
3. On your signal, encourage both your child and dog to race through the tunnel as fast as they can.
4. Celebrate when they reach the other end of the tunnel.
5. Repeat the race, trying to beat their previous times and adding fun challenges along the way.

Snack Toss

Snack Toss is a game that improves your dog's catching skills and hand-eye coordination for your child.

- *How many persons can be involved:* This activity typically involves a child tossing treats or toys for the dog.
- *Can it be played by a child alone:* Yes, a child can play this game alone by tossing treats or toys for the dog.
- *What you'll need:* Dog-friendly treats or small toys.

Instructions:

1. Have your child stand a short distance away from your dog, holding a treat or toy.
2. Encourage your child to toss the treat or toy gently towards your dog.
3. Your dog should catch the treat or retrieve the toy in their mouth.
4. Praise and reward your dog for successfully catching or retrieving the item.
5. Gradually increase the distance and challenge your dog's catching abilities.

Toy Fetch Relay

Set up a relay race where your child and dog take turns fetching toys and bringing them back to a designated spot.

- *How many persons can be involved:* This activity involves a child and a dog.
- *Can it be played by a child alone:* No, this activity requires supervision to ensure safety and proper coordination between the child and the dog.
- *What you'll need:* Dog toys and a designated spot for returning the toys.

Instructions:

1. Have your child and dog stand at opposite ends of the room.
2. Give your child a toy and instruct them to throw it to your dog.
3. Encourage your dog to fetch the toy and bring it back to the designated spot.
4. Celebrate when they successfully complete the relay, and then switch roles.
5. Time each relay race to add an element of friendly competition.

Stuffed Animal Tag

Use a stuffed animal as the "tagger" in a game of tag between your child and dog.

- *How many persons can be involved:* This activity involves a child and a dog.
- *Can it be played by a child alone:* No, this activity requires supervision to ensure safety and proper coordination between the child and the dog.
- *What you'll need:* A stuffed animal.

Instructions:

1. Select a stuffed animal to be the "tagger" and have your child hold it.
2. Encourage your child to tag your dog with the stuffed animal, initiating a game of chase.
3. Once your dog is tagged, they can then become the "tagger" and chase your child.
4. Ensure that everyone plays gently and safely, avoiding rough movements or excessive chasing.

Doggie Dress-Up

Doggie Dress-Up is a game that involves your child dressing up your dog in fun costumes or accessories.

- *How many persons can be involved:* This activity involves a child dressing up the dog.
- *Can it be played by a child alone:* Yes, a child can play this game alone with the dog.
- *What you'll need:* Dog-friendly costumes or accessories.

Instructions:

1. Gather a selection of dog-friendly costumes or accessories.
2. Have your child choose a costume or accessory and help them dress up your dog.
3. Take pictures and make it a fun photo session.
4. Ensure your dog is comfortable and not stressed by the outfits.
5. Enjoy the bonding experience and share laughs as you dress up your dog together.

Measuring Progress and Adjusting Your Dog's Mental Stimulation Routine

Creating a mental stimulation routine for your beloved canine companion is a wonderful way to keep them engaged, happy, and mentally sharp.

However, just like with any routine, it's crucial to monitor your dog's progress and be ready to make adjustments as needed. Dogs, much like humans, have diverse needs, abilities, and interests that can evolve over time.

Here, we'll explore why measuring progress is important, how to assess your dog's development, signs that the routine needs adjustment, and effective ways to modify their mental stimulation regimen.

Why Measuring Progress Is Crucial

- **Assessing Engagement:** Monitoring your dog's behavior during mental exercises allows you to gauge their level of interest and engagement. An enthusiastic dog is more likely to benefit from the activities you provide.

- **Preventing Boredom:** Dogs can grow bored with repetitive tasks or activities that are too easy. Tracking progress helps you recognize when changes are necessary to keep their minds stimulated.

- **Evaluating Health:** Changes in behavior or a decrease in enthusiasm could be early signs of health issues. By measuring progress, you can catch these signs early and seek veterinary care if needed.

- **Adapting to Development:** Dogs go through various life stages, each with its own mental and physical capabilities. Tracking progress helps you adjust the routine to suit your dog's current developmental needs.

How to Measure Progress

1. **Observe Behavior:** Pay close attention to how your dog reacts during mental exercises. Note if they are excited, focused, frustrated, or disinterested. Keeping a journal can help track patterns.

2. **Completion Time:** Record how long it takes your dog to complete certain tasks or puzzles. Consistently quick finishes or prolonged times might indicate the need for adjustment.

3. **Skill Improvement:** Notice if your dog is getting better at tasks like obedience commands, puzzle-solving, or learning new tricks. Improved performance indicates progress.

4. **Energy Levels:** Before and after mental exercises, observe your dog's energy levels. They should feel content and satisfied after the activities, not overly tired or restless.

5. **Interest Levels:** Take note of which activities spark your dog's enthusiasm. If they seem uninterested in certain tasks or toys, it may be time to try something new.

Signs That the Routine Needs Adjustment

- **Boredom or Restlessness:** If your dog appears disinterested or restless during activities, it's a clear indicator that the routine lacks engagement.

- **Frustration:** Continuous failure to complete puzzles or tasks can lead to frustration. Simplify exercises or provide more guidance if your dog seems consistently frustrated.

- **Disinterest:** Loss of interest in activities they once enjoyed suggests the need for new challenges or different types of mental stimulation.

- **Decreased Enthusiasm:** If your dog shows less excitement during play or training sessions, it might be time to introduce more engaging activities.

- **Health Issues:** Sudden changes in behavior, such as lethargy, decreased appetite, or unusual aggression, could indicate underlying health concerns. Consult with your vet if you notice these signs.

How to Adjust the Routine Effectively

1. **Identify the Problem:** Pinpoint which aspects of the routine need adjustment. Is it the difficulty level, the type of activity, or the frequency of exercises?

2. **Gradual Changes:** Implement modifications gradually rather than all at once. Introduce one or two adjustments to assess their impact on your dog.

3. **Replace or Rotate Activities:** Retire activities that no longer engage your dog and introduce new ones. For instance, swap out an old puzzle toy for a different type or rotate various toys to maintain interest.

4. **Adapt Difficulty Levels:** Adjust the complexity of puzzles and training exercises based on your dog's progress. As they improve, gradually increase the difficulty to keep them challenged.

5. **Vary the Routine:** Incorporate a mix of activities such as obedience training, scent work, physical exercises, and interactive play. A diverse routine keeps things fresh and exciting.

6. **Consider Age and Health:** Your dog's age and health should guide adjustments to the routine. Puppies, adult dogs, and seniors have different needs and capabilities.

7. **Seek Professional Help:** If your dog continues to struggle or shows persistent behavioral issues, consider consulting a professional dog trainer or behaviorist for guidance.

Sample Scenario: Adjusting the Routine

Let's imagine a scenario with a sample adjustment for your dog's mental stimulation routine:

Scenario: You've been giving your adult Labrador puzzle toys for mental stimulation. Lately, you've noticed that they solve these puzzles quite quickly, indicating a need for more challenging activities.

Adjustment:

1. **Identify the Problem:** The puzzle toys are no longer providing enough mental stimulation.

2. **Gradual Change:** Introduce more complex puzzle toys gradually to increase the challenge level.

3. **Replace Activities:** Instead of the usual puzzle toys, try introducing interactive treat-dispensing balls or toys with multiple compartments.

4. **Adapt Difficulty:** Choose puzzles with varying difficulty levels to keep your Labrador engaged and challenged.

5. **Vary the Routine:** In addition to puzzles, incorporate scent work games, obedience training sessions with new commands, and interactive playtime.

By making these adjustments, you're ensuring that your dog remains mentally engaged, challenged, and happy during their mental stimulation routine. Remember to observe their behavior, track progress, and be open to further modifications as your dog's needs evolve over time.

BONUS

THE BEST 5 RECIPES FOR THE HEALTH OF YOUR DOG FRIEND

Chapter 3
Conclusion

As we conclude our exploration into the world of mental exercise for dogs, it becomes clear that engaging our furry companions in stimulating activities goes far beyond mere entertainment—it is a pathway to achieving optimal psychophysical well-being. Throughout this journey, we have delved into the diverse facets of canine intelligence, understanding how each type contributes to our dogs' problem-solving abilities, adaptability, and social interactions. Now, let us reflect on the significance of mental exercise and its profound impact on our canine companions' lives.

Achieving Psychophysical Well-Being

Physical activity and play are not just about burning off excess energy; they are vital components in ensuring our dogs' overall health and happiness. By engaging in mental exercises tailored to their intelligence strengths, we provide our dogs with avenues to explore their natural instincts, sharpen their cognitive skills, and maintain a balanced emotional state. This holistic approach to well-being extends beyond the physical realm, nurturing their mental acuity and emotional stability.

The Role of the Family Unit

Within the family unit, dogs find a sense of belonging, love, and companionship that is fundamental to their well-being. As integral members of our households, they thrive on the bonds we share and the activities we engage in together. However, it is equally important to encourage socialization beyond the family context. By exposing our dogs to new environments, people, and experiences, we help broaden their horizons and develop their social intelligence. This, in turn, fosters a well-rounded dog who is confident, adaptable, and at ease in various situations.

Encouraging Responsibility and Peace

Having a healthy and dynamic dog as a companion is a joy that comes with responsibilities. Through mental exercises and training, we not only enhance their skills but also instill in them a sense of discipline and obedience. This lays the foundation for a harmonious relationship based on mutual understanding and respect. Furthermore, the peace that comes from a well-trained and mentally stimulated dog extends beyond the household. It influences our interactions with others, as a content and balanced dog is more likely to exhibit calm and friendly behavior in social settings.

As you continue your journey of caring for your dog's mental health, I encourage you to explore resources available online, such as websites, apps, or support groups dedicated to dog training and enrichment. These platforms offer valuable insights, tips, and techniques to enhance your dog's mental stimulation and overall quality of life.

Lastly, I invite you to share your experiences and progress in the field of dog training and mental exercise. Your feedback and insights are invaluable in fostering a community of responsible and informed dog owners. By leaving a review or opinion on the book, you contribute to the collective knowledge and understanding of canine well-being, benefiting both current and future dog owners alike.

In conclusion, by prioritizing mental exercise alongside physical activity, you can ensure that your dog leads a fulfilling and enriching life, characterized by optimal health, happiness, and companionship. Thank you for your dedication to the well-being of your furry friend, and may your journey together be filled with joy, learning, and countless shared adventures.

Made in the USA
Monee, IL
06 January 2025

76200027R00052